In a League of Their Own!

About the author

Gail Newsham was born in Preston in 1953, just a stone's throw from the Dick, Kerr works. She has an abiding love of football and, as a youngster, used to play in the street with the lads.

She began playing for Preston Rangers when she was nineteen years old. She was a competent left-back with the team and won many honours while playing in the North West Women's Regional Football League. Gail was an active member of the League management committee for many years, holding almost every officer's position between 1981 and 1992, and in 1993 she was presented with a special award by the League in recognition of her services to women's football. In 1986 she was responsible for setting up the Lancashire Trophy, an international women's soccer tournament, which has attracted teams from Austria, Germany, Sweden, Switzerland, Eire, Scotland and all parts of England. The event is exclusive to women's football and is now regarded as the best of its kind in the country.

It was not until 1992, while organizing a reunion of Dick, Kerr Ladies at the Lancashire Trophy as part of the Preston Guild celebrations, that it occurred to her that there was no official record of the team's history, and that unless something was done quickly, their story would die with them and be lost for ever. Learning about the team and their remarkable successes made her all the more determined that their story should be told. As a Prestonian, she is very proud of the team's origins and feels that the Dick, Kerr Ladies fully deserve the recognition this book will bring them.

In a League of Their Own!
The Dick, Kerr Ladies' Football Club

Gail J. Newsham

Scarlet Press

For truth and honesty

First published by Pride of Place Publishing, 1994
This edition published by Scarlet Press
5 Montague Road, London E8 2HN

British Library Cataloguing in Publication Data
A catalogue record for this book is available from
the British Library

ISBN   1 85727 029 0 pb

Designed and produced for Scarlet Press by
Chase Production Services, Chadlington, OX7 3LN
Typeset from the author's disk by
Stanford DTP Services, Northampton
Printed in the EC by J.W. Arrowsmith, Bristol

Contents

List of Illustrations

Foreword

In 1937, I was serving my plumber's apprenticeship at a firm which was next door to the fruit shop owned by Alfred Frankland, the manager of Dick, Kerr Ladies FC. It was thought at the time that women's football was something new, but of course this was wrong, as they were already twenty years down the road when I first heard about them.

I always took an interest in the team and was kept in touch with what was happening with them, and I knew even in those days that they travelled all over the country playing the game and that they were a very successful team. I remember being invited to referee at several of their matches and being presented to the girls. There wasn't very much women's football played in those days and to actually see them play was quite remarkable. Some of them were very good players and they always had big crowds at their games. I knew that the Football Association did not look very kindly upon them, and it was thought that we, as professional players, should not encourage the women's games. I personally couldn't see that they were doing any harm, especially when they were helping so many people by raising such a lot of money for charity.

But that's all behind them now. The FA are supporting women's football and it is fast becoming a world sport. Perhaps this is due in some way to the determination of Dick, Kerr Ladies, who played on after the FA ban and helped lay the foundations for today's game. The high reputation of Preston (Dick, Kerr) Ladies was well deserved, and coming from Preston myself, I can feel proud of their successful history. *In a League of Their Own!* is a fitting tribute to all they achieved.

Acknowledgements

My sincere gratitude goes to my family, for their unconditional love and their eternal support for whatever I try to do. To Dad, Mum, Pat and Andy, I don't know what I would do without you. My love and thanks also to the many friends who have supported me during the past few up-and-down years: to June Gregson, Liz Whittall, Chris Hill, Lorraine Carrington, Cath O'Sullivan, Rebecca and Stephanie Brindle, Pat Rogers and Ann Smith, thanks for listening, but above all, thanks for caring. Thanks also to Maggie, Janet and Lesley. I know I couldn't have done it without you. To Sheila D. Ferguson, my very special friend, my love to you always. Last, but not least, to Val Davies, my love and thanks for all the same reasons this time around. It's just as important now as it was then.

Preface

Since 1986 I had been involved in organizing a two-day International Women's Soccer Tournament, the Lancashire Trophy. It had always been our belief that the Lancashire Trophy was more than just another soccer tournament, and it was exclusive to women's football. We felt that this competition was the best in Europe. The theme of the entire weekend was 'Football, Friendship and Fun', and it was our aim to provide as much of each as we could. Over the years we had teams from Austria, Switzerland, Germany, Sweden, Eire, Scotland and England competing for the trophy.

The residential teams would arrive on a Friday evening, and after welcoming everyone to the competition, we would entertain them with a Karaoke night. The idea was that a good old sing-song would help to break the ice and enable everyone to become better acquainted. Football would be played all day on Saturday and we would provide entertainment for everyone in the evening. The football would resume again on Sunday, building up to the final of the competition. Afterwards, we staged a gala presentation evening with a star cabaret and disco, when everyone would join together in celebrating the end of a superb weekend. It was a wonderful atmosphere which captured the true spirit of what the tournament had come to represent.

Preston Guild year fell in 1992 and the tournament was included in the long list of the year's Guild events. It was the first time that a women's soccer tournament had been recognized in the official Guild calendar. Given the history of women's football in Preston, and the prestige of our competition having Guild status, it seemed to be the appropriate time to try to stage a reunion of the world-famous Dick, Kerr Ladies.

Preston Guild occurs only once every twenty years, and ex-Prestonians living in all four corners of the world return to their home town for these unique week-long celebrations. It is a historic event dating back to medieval times. In 1179 King Henry II granted a charter to Preston, and this privilege was renewed in further charters granted by later kings and queens of England. The Preston Guild Merchant was initially set up to protect traders in the town from outside competition. Anyone who wanted to trade in Preston had to be a member of the Guild Merchant or suffer the consequences. Members of the Guild would meet to discuss official business, but at the same time they would combine it with pleasure. Consequently, this was seen to be an occasion of civic celebration and great festivity.

Since then, Preston has celebrated this historical charter with all kinds of trade fairs, pageants, processions, carnivals, concerts and street parties all over the town. There is a terrific atmosphere and a great community spirit everywhere you go, as 'Proud Preston' really lives up to its name.

In the spring of 1991, I had by chance met a former Dick, Kerr Ladies player, Brenda Eastwood, at another local women's football competition staged at Bamber Bridge FC, near Preston. Brenda was there to present trophies to the winners of the tournament, and I invited her to present the awards at the Lancashire Trophy a few months later. Formerly Brenda Keen, her dream of playing football for Dick, Kerr Ladies was realized when, against all the odds, she played for the team in the first post-war fixture, on Good Friday 1946. She made her debut in goal in the match played at Glossop in front of a crowd of 5,000.

Brenda had been born with a heart defect which dramatically affected her school life, and her parents were warned of the possibility that she might die. After years of medical supervision, however, she was given a clean bill of health at nineteen and never looked back. Brenda did, though, suffer a serious heart attack in January 1993, but made a marvellous recovery. In 1994, at the age of seventy-one, she was awarded a bursary at the University of Central Lancashire to study for a degree in Accountancy, Business Information Systems and Physiology. The Winifred Keen Bursary was only awarded once every two years to women over the age of sixty, and Brenda was chosen from six other hopeful candidates. Brenda said: 'I decided to do something with the rest of my life after I suffered the heart attack. It was a traumatic experience. Being selected to receive the bursary has been a great honour for me.'

As a result of meeting Brenda I had the idea of trying to organize a reunion of former Dick, Kerr Ladies players for Preston Guild year. As the Guild occurs so seldom, I thought that the 1992 Guild celebrations were likely to be the last opportunity they would have to be together at such a special time in Preston's history. I asked

Brenda if she knew the whereabouts of any other members of the team so that we could try to get things moving. All she had was a telephone number for Joan Burke. I rang Joan, explained what I was trying to do, and asked could I call round to talk with her about it.

Joan Burke (Tich) began playing for the team in 1939, when she was fourteen. She lived on Marsh Lane and was kicking a ball about more or less as soon as she could walk. She was spotted playing football at Coulthard's foundry, in a cinder yard, when she was very young by Alice Kell, the first player to be captain of Dick, Kerr Ladies in 1917. Alice had watched Joan's skills develop over the years and she knew that Joan would be an ideal player for her former team as soon as she was old enough.

Tich had a few old photographs from her days with the team and I was fascinated by them. The sheer size of the crowds on the photographs in comparison with today's game was amazing. I borrowed one of the team photos and contacted the local paper to see if they could help to locate more players. This turned out to be very successful.

As a result of this publicity, I went to see Frances Appleby, who first played for the team in 1946 and had a couple of old newspaper clippings. It was lovely to talk with Frances and I was overwhelmed by the match reports she had carefully saved over the years. The *Daily Herald* had covered Dick, Kerr's games; I had had no idea that they had received so much media attention.

I soon came to realize that there had been nothing officially written down about these wonderful ladies and that, if something were not done soon, their story would be lost for ever.

The next lady I visited was Edna Clayton. Now seventy-eight, Edna had played for Dick, Kerr's in the early 1930s. Unfortunately, she had suffered a slight stroke some years earlier which had affected her memory, so she could remember little of her days with the team, but she took me to meet Lydia Ackers, who was eighty-eight years old and living in a residential home for elderly gentlefolk. Lydia was a bright old lady, eager to share her memories of those far-off days. Her eyes were shining as she remembered her time playing football in the 1920s. 'We were famous, you see, and everybody wanted to see us,' she said.

Sadly, Lydia passed away in 1993 after a fall. She was ninety. Fortunately I had tape-recorded my interviews with her, as I had done with all the ladies I met – Joan Whalley, Alice Barlow, Nancy Thomson, Jean Latham, Elsie Yates, Joan Burke and Frances

Appleby – so I have managed to save all their memories for posterity.

During the two years spent researching the history of Dick, Kerr Ladies FC, I was fortunate to be given scrapbooks belonging to Joan Whalley and Alfred Frankland/Kath Latham. The information contained in them has been an invaluable source in putting this book together. I also made contact with a gentleman in Canada, Colin José. He copied newspaper reports for me from the *New York Times*, the *Fall River Globe* and the *Fall River Evening Herald*. I also spent hour after hour in the reference library at the Harris Museum in Preston, where the *Lancashire Daily Post* is kept on reels of film. Bert Stanley allowed me to see his mother Alice's diaries from the 1920s, also an invaluable source of information. Without all their help, a truly extraordinary story of a unique women's football team might never have been told.

1 From Factory Yard Football to Playing at Deepdale

Around the turn of the century, women's attitudes to their place in society were beginning to change – they were 'coming out of the kitchen' and wanted to contribute more to the order of things. Women wanted to work, they wanted to vote and they wanted to play, and they were no longer prepared to accept that they were inferior to the male population. To many women, the Victorian values of simply expecting them to marry and have children were no longer acceptable. The Suffragette movement was proof that women wanted the right to determine their own lives; women's standing in the world was about to change for ever.

The outbreak of war in 1914 meant that these changes were not only desired but necessary. While the men were away fighting for king and country on the battlefields of Europe, the demand for weapons, ammunition, food and medical supplies had to be met, and on the home front women all over the country were playing their part in the war effort. Many women were already familiar with working in factories, but during the war the amount of manual labour undertaken by women increased sharply as more and more of them were needed to help keep the war machine alive. A new comradeship between women was being born.

The firm of Dick, Kerr and Co. Ltd was named after its two Scottish founders, W. B. Dick and John Kerr of Kilmarnock. Around the turn of the century, they bought the Strand Road site to produce tramway and light railway equipment, and this formed the nucleus of the present traction works at Preston, now known as GEC Alsthom Traction Ltd. The company became the leading British firm for the traction industry and they were responsible for the electrification of railway from Liverpool to Southport in 1904. They expanded rapidly and activities at Preston included the building of 8,350 tram cars for this country and for major cities throughout the world. The factory turned its attention to the production of ammunition at the outbreak of the First World War.

It has always been thought that Alfred Frankland was the founder of Dick, Kerr Ladies Football Club, but the real credit for that must go to Grace Sibbert, who got the ball rolling by being the instigator at the factory of a women's team.

Women's football was not unheard of, and the first recorded ladies' football match took place at the Crouch End Athletic Ground in north London, on Saturday 23 March 1895, when the British Ladies Football Club, whose secretary and captain was Miss Nettie Honeyball, organized a game between the north and south of London. Nettie must have been considered a little eccentric, as in the late 1800s she saw no reason why women should not be allowed to participate in more physical sports and consequently advertised to find girls to play 'a manly game and show that it could be womanly as well'.* They practised on a pitch close to the Alexandra Palace racecourse.

Nettie, however, was not the only forward-thinking member of the club. The club's president was Lady Florence Dixie. She was the youngest daughter of the Marquess of Queensberry and was reputed to be the first female war correspondent. She was an excellent horeswoman and also extremely useful with a rifle.

The result of the Crouch End match was a 7–1 victory for north London, and although the footballing skills of both teams left a lot to be desired, they showed enthusiasm for the game even though they were reported to have forgotten the rules and did not even change ends at half time.

During the 1914–18 war, ladies' football teams were being formed up and down the country as a means of raising much-needed funds for many worthy causes, but the north of England saw the game flourish more quickly than it did in other parts of the land. As for the ladies of Dick, Kerr and Co. Ltd in Preston, little did they realize what sort of impact their contribution would have on the rest of the world.

During their tea breaks and lunch times, the girls would often join in with the apprentices having a kick around in the factory yard, and Grace was an ever-present member during these footballing frolics. During the October of 1917, the men's football team had been having a run of bad results. They had played a match at the weekend and suffered yet another heavy defeat. The

* *Daily Graphic*, March 1895.

following week, the team were taking some flak from Grace and her pals in the staff canteen. 'Call yourselves a football team?' they said, 'You're useless; we could do better than you lot!' Some of the lads were a bit embarrassed by the girls' jibes, so they challenged them to prove their skills in a proper match. Grace took up the challenge immediately and said to her workmates, 'Come on then, girls, let's have a go.'

Arrangements were made accordingly and a match was played on a field somewhere in the Penwortham area of Preston. Although there is no record of the result of this game, it was obviously a very enjoyable pursuit for the ladies because they decided to continue with their newly-formed football team. And so began an extraordinary venture into the sporting arena for these otherwise unremarkable working-class girls from Preston.

The first ever photograph of the Dick, Kerr Ladies in their famous black-and-white strip shows Grace on the front row, second from the left. She was told that as she had got it all started she could keep the match ball. She was naturally delighted at the gesture and made sure that the ball was with her for the team photograph.

Grace was born on 13 October 1891 and married John James Sibbert (Jimmy) on 29 November 1913. Jimmy joined the Loyal North Lancashire Regiment and fought on the Somme in France during the war. (The Battle of the Somme was one of the great offensives of the First World War. It began on 1 July 1916 and continued until the end of November. The British and French armies attacked the German positions on a battle front of twenty-five miles. The total British losses in this great battle were almost 500,000 men.) Jimmy was captured and taken prisoner and suffered at the hands of the Germans in one of the prisoner-of-war camps. Grace, meanwhile, had been drafted to work at Dick, Kerr's in munitions as part of the war effort, and as the ladies began playing matches for charity, Grace had a deeply personal incentive to help the war effort: her husband Jimmy's terrible experiences in the German POW camps. Unfortunately, however, ill health was to prevent her from taking an active part as a regular member of the team.

Not long after the October match against the men, with Christmas just around the corner, the matron of the Moor Park Military Hospital in Preston asked the girls at Dick, Kerr's if they would help the hospital by doing some concerts to raise much-needed funds to provide better care for the patients. (The Moor

The first ever team photo, October 1917. Grace Sibbert with the ball.

Park Hospital was established to treat personnel wounded during the First World War. It was originally no more than an agricultural pavilion and it was extended several times, eventually including an operating theatre. The hospital remained in use until March 1919.) The girls were only too happy to help, but decided that a more novel way to raise money would be to arrange a charity football match instead of a concert.

Exactly when Alfred Frankland took the helm and got involved with the team is not known, but it must have been shortly after their first footballing exploits. He worked at Dick, Kerr's as a draughtsman in No. 6 Department Office, and it is thought that, from his office window, he saw the ladies playing football in the works yard. He obviously saw a great potential waiting to be nurtured. No one can deny that his guidance, dedication and organizational skills were an invaluable contribution to the history of women's football.

The first match organized to raise funds for Moor Park Hospital was with the neighbouring Arundel Coulthard Foundry on Marsh Lane. The ladies at the foundry had accepted the challenge and arrangements were made for the game to be played at Deepdale, the home of Preston North End (PNE). At a meeting held on 6 November 1917, the North End board granted permission for the game to go ahead and resolved that a charge of £5 be made for the use of the ground. Any monies received would be given to charity. They agreed to advertise the match on PNE posters with the ladies' clubs paying a proportion of the cost. On 13 November 1917, the board must have been in a more generous mood, as they rescinded the £5 charge. The match was given quite a high profile and was advertised in the local paper as being a 'Great Holiday Attraction'.

Christmas Day 1917 thus saw the start of what was to be the most phenomenal success story in the history of women's sport. In front of 10,000 people, Dick, Kerr Ladies notched up the first of many famous victories, and raised in excess of £600 for wounded soldiers at the Moor Park Military Hospital. Assuming money doubles in value every ten years, the £600 raised in 1917 would be worth £153,600 in 1997, an enormous sum for one ladies' football match. Ironically, their first score line was the same as in their last ever game, played against Handy Angles in 1965: Dick, Kerr Ladies 4, Arundel Coulthard Foundry 0. The team on that historic day lined up as follows: E. Clayton, B. Traynor,

E. Nixon, E. Birkins, Alice Kell (captain), M. Kay, A. Standing, G. Whittle, F. Rance, Florrie Redford, Lily Jones.

The Coulthard's team played in red-and-white stripes and Dick, Kerr Ladies played in black-and-white stripes with the addition of natty close-fitting hats to match, described in the *Lancashire Daily Post* of 27 December. The wearing of corsets was barred and the game was refereed by Mr John Lewis of Blackburn.

The match report in the *Daily Post* reads:

> After their Christmas dinner the crowd were in the right humour for enjoying this distinctly war-time novelty. There was a tendency amongst the players at the start to giggle, but they soon settled down to the game in earnest. Dick, Kerr's were not long in showing that they suffered less than their opponents from stage fright, and they had a better all round idea of the game. Woman for woman they were also speedier, and had a larger share of that quality which in football slang is known as 'heftiness'. Quite a number of their shots at goal would not have disgraced the regular professional except in direction, and even professionals have been known on occasion to be a trifle wide of the target. Their forward work, indeed, was often surprisingly good, one or two of the ladies displaying quite admirable ball control, whilst combination was by no means a negligible quality. Coulthard's were strongest in defence, the backs battling against long odds, never giving in, and the goalkeeper doing remarkably well, but the forwards, who were understood to have sadly disappointed their friends, were clearly affected with nerves.

All the conventions were duly honoured. The teams, on making their appearance (after being photographed), indulged in 'shooting in' and the rival captains, before tossing the coin for choice of ends, shook hands in the approved manner. At first the spectators were inclined to treat the game with a little too much levity, and they found amusement in almost everything, from the pace (which until they got used to it had the same effect as a slow-moving Kinema-picture), to the 'how dare you' expression of a player when she was pushed by an opponent. But when they saw that the ladies meant business, and were 'playing the game', they readily took up the correct attitude and impartially cheered and encouraged each side. Within five minutes Dick, Kerr's had scored through Whittle, and before half time they added further goals by Birkins, a fine shot from fifteen yards out, just under the bar, and Rance. Coulthard's, who were quite out of the picture in the first half, 'bucked up' after the interval, and deserved a goal, but it was denied them, much to the disappointment of the spectators. They had a rare opportunity from a penalty in the last few minutes, but the ball was kicked straight at the keeper. On the other hand, Dick, Kerr's added to their score, Rance running through and netting while the opposition backs were 'arguing' about some alleged offence, a natural touch which greatly delighted the onlookers. John Lewis refereed with discretion, keeping within the laws, though he was clearly in a dilemma, probably for the first time in his official career, when one of the players was 'winded' by the ball.

Following the success of this match, further matches were organized with the intention of raising money for charity, to help ease the suffering of servicemen and their families affected by the war. Such was the scale of this suffering on the bloody battlefields of war-torn Europe that few families were left untouched by the conflict. The demand placed upon charitable organizations at the time was consequently at saturation point and so the new wave of ladies playing football for charity met with great enthusiasm. Ladies' football was without doubt a growing spectator sport. The novelty aspect probably played a big part initially, but the skill and enthusiasm of the girls giving their all for charity, and for their sport, was enough to ensure they gained the respect of the public, not only for their fund-raising efforts, but also for their skill on the field. Dick, Kerr Ladies were fast becoming famous, in demand, and they enjoyed their new-found celebrity status. They did, of course, receive a great deal of support and encouragement from the management at Dick, Kerr and Co. Ltd, who were happy that the ladies' success meant free advertising for the company wherever they played.

It was not all plain sailing, however. There were those who were totally opposed to the whole idea of ladies playing football. Many thought that the female frame was not built for such a rough game, and that playing football could cause damage to women's health. Others felt merely that the game was not suitable for ladies simply because it did not fit in with what they thought a woman's role in life was meant to be. The anti-ladies' football lobby often voiced negative opinions, but it is difficult to identity the genuine causes of their objection. Women were playing football without suffering any ill effects, and the public were obviously keen to watch them play. Why, then, such vehement opposition?

By 1918, as a result of the war effort, it was hard to imagine a single job not taken over by women. From operating the most complicated machinery to work in the equally important and skilful work of farming – there were women in every position. They could even be seen lugging hundredweight sacks of coal out of the mines on their backs (a small concession to their sex was the introduction of the hundredweight sack instead of the usual two-hundredweight variety).

Molly Walker, who played for Dick, Kerr's at that time, was treated as an outcast by her boyfriend's family because they didn't approve of her wearing shorts and showing her legs. This attitude was typical of the time and it is therefore all the more amazing that Dick, Kerr Ladies achieved the success that they did.

Following the Deepdale match, the ladies' committee applied for use of the ground for a game to be played on 23 February 1918, and another on Easter Monday. Permission was granted by the board on the following conditions: 'we take charge of the gate and pay over to Dick, Kerr and Co. 80 per cent of the net gate, that is after all expenses incidental to the match are paid'.

It is important to emphasize the support and co-operation given to ladies' football at this time from the male bastion of soccer. The North End board were more than supportive to Dick, Kerr Ladies Football Club, given that this was early 1918, the world was fighting a bloody war, and women's rights were not on anyone's agenda.

It is clear that ladies' football had been quickly recognized as a means of making money, and not only from the charitable aspect of the game. It is obvious from the North End board meetings that they saw the ladies' matches held at Deepdale as profitable. The large crowds attracted to the Dick, Kerr matches also generated revenue from the sale of refreshments at the ground, and so it was beneficial for all concerned for Deepdale to be the ladies' team 'home' venue.

On 26 February the game planned for Easter Monday was rearranged for Good Friday, and use of the ground was also allowed for a game to be played on 9 March. Both games were played on the same terms as the match played on 23 February, 80 per cent of the gate receipts being paid to Dick, Kerr & Co. Ltd.

On Good Friday, 29 March 1918, the Dick, Kerr's team took on Bolton Ladies, notching up another victory with a 5–1 scoreline.

Kicking off the match was nine-year-old Judith Todd. The invitation to kick off the game originally went out to Judith's mother, a prominent local figure in Liberal politics and war charities and a suitably distinguished female to officiate at the match. Perhaps Mrs Todd thought it highly undignified, as well as almost physically impossible, to stand in the middle of a footballing arena and kick a ball while wearing the long skirts of the period. Whatever the reason, her daughter, Judith was offered as a replacement.

Now living in London, Judith remembers being very excited at the prospect and she hoped to be allowed to wear a pair of blue shorts like the Dick, Kerr Ladies. But this was forbidden, and her final strip was a short navy skirt and white jersey.

'You're to come off directly you've kicked it,' said her father. 'You're not to stay and play. Do you understand?' Judith was rather disappointed, but was more enthusiastic after her father gave her a short lesson in the garden on the correct way to kick a football.

Children of that era were not encouraged to think too highly of themselves, and it was not until some thirty years later that her mother showed her a letter received from Alfred Frankland, saying that she had 'performed her duties in an excellent manner in such a way that pleased the crowd'.

Dick, Kerr's players were obviously keen to keep up the momentum of their winning start and saw the need to practise as a means of becoming fitter and faster than their opponents. The charitable nature of the games was commendable and they wanted to do everything they could to help the needy, but it is none the less clear that these ladies wanted to play football, they wanted to win, and their aim was to be the best.

By the close of the 1917–18 season, the ladies had played four matches at Deepdale and although the records on gate receipts are sketchy they were attracting significant numbers of spectators.

25 Dec 1917	DK v. Coulthard's 4–0	crowd 10,000 – gate £600
23 Feb 1918	DK v. Lancaster 1–1	crowd 5,000 – gate ?
9 Mar 1918	DK v. Barrow 2–0	crowd 2,000 – gate ?
29 Mar 1918	DK v. Bolton 5–1	crowd 6,000 – gate £200

In May of 1918, an application made from Dick, Kerr Ladies to practise at Deepdale was granted by the board, and later in the year, in August, the ground was offerd to them on the following terms: £12 for a Saturday match; £3 per week for training on Tuesday,

Wednesday and Thursday of each week during the daytime. Special arrangements to be made for holiday fixtures.

By the start of the new season, Dick, Kerr's had once again approached the North End board for use of the Deepdale ground. Extracts from the minutes are as follows:

27 August 1918

Resolved that Dick, Kerr Ladies Football Club could rent Deepdale for season 1918/19 on the following terms:

1. £12 for a Saturday match with Dick, Kerr's agreeing to take the ground for at least ten matches.

2. £20 for Christmas Day.

3. £1 a week for training three days a week on Tuesday, Wednesday and Thursday during the daytime. The renting of the ground for training for the whole season or any part thereof is at Dick, Kerr's option. Payment to be made on the Monday following each match.

In an article published in the *Lancashire Daily Post* on 31 August 1918, headed 'LADIES FOOTBALL JUSTIFIED', it is interesting to note the sentiments of the reporter:

> When munition girls began to invade the football field, some of the old shell-backs scoffed at their usefulness both in a playing sense and as an attraction, and not even the fact that they were devoting their energies to the help of War charities seemed to abate the objections in some quarters. In Preston, the movement has been fostered instead of decried, and in the Dick, Kerr's eleven we have had perhaps the best ladies' team in the country. The girls have had the benefit of enthusiastic sponsors and capable mentors, and the balance sheet of their last season's activities, furnished me by Mr A. Frankland, to whom much of the success is due, is a convincing answer to those who derided or frowned upon their football existence. The statement shows that the fine sum of £804 10s 5d was raised, and that after amusement tax of £105 4s 7d, and rent of ground amounting to £61 4s 1d had been paid, together with general expenses that are eminently moderate, a net balance of £553 17s 1d remained. Of this £338 1s was

Training at Deepdale, 1918.
Left to right: Jessie Walmsley, Flo Redford, Alice Kell, Molly
Walker, unknown, unknown, Jennie Harris.

given in July as a donation to the Moor Park hospital, and now £190 16s 1d of the residue has been divided amongst the War charities. The lump sum handed over to the Moor Park hospital consisted of the proceeds of the match with Coulthard's team at Christmas, in connection with which no expenses were paid, and it should be added that a further sum of £150, which does not appear in the accounts, was given to the hospital by the firm of Dick, Kerr & Co.

This financial result can only be described as magnificent, and a tribute to those who have organised the team and have played in it. It is not necessary to consider here and now whether ladies' football will survive the War. The point is that it is serving an altogether admirable purpose at the moment. I know that if one of the recognised League clubs had raised such a sum for charity it would have regarded it, and quite legitimately so, as a great achievement. How much more so, then, a body of girls who combine a means of exercise and relaxation from their arduous work, a means of helping a number of splendid charities? In the light of such a result, it is good to know that the club is going forward this season with greater zest and better prospects than before.

Already there are questions arising from the figures quoted, the answers to which one can only ponder. We shall look at this in more detail later, but the first observation is this: the general expenses quoted by Mr Frankland on the balance sheet amount to approximately £85. Can this really be considered as 'eminently moderate'? If we again work on the principle of money doubling in value every ten years, that £85 in 1917 would be worth something like £21,500 in 1997. Second, if £800 was raised from the two games against Coulthard's and Bolton, is it feasible that the remaining sum – a mere £4 10s 5d – was raised from the other two games against Lancaster and Barrow, with a combined gate of 7,000 people?

The start of the new season, 1918–19, saw the ladies attract a 'big crowd' at Deepdale for their match against Vickers of Barrow. They continued their unbeaten run, recording a 1–0 victory over the Barrow side, with a goal scored by Molly Walker, their new signing from Lancaster Ladies.

The *Lancashire Daily Post* of 23 February 1918 was of the opinion that there was 'distinctly a public for ladies' football'. Certainly

Dick, Kerr Ladies were building up quite a following, attracting good crowds to all their matches. Alice Kell and Florrie Redford were emerging as two very skilful players, frequently mentioned in the match reports. The management of the team were keen to recruit talented lady footballers to help Dick, Kerr Ladies become the best and to raise more charity money, and they were consequently always on the look-out for new players.

On 9 October 1918, however, the team suffered their first defeat at the hands of Whitehaven Ladies. The match, played at Deepdale in front of a large crowd, was one of the few defeats throughout their history. They were beaten 2–0.

Thankfully, November saw the end of the war. The guns fell silent and the peace treaty was signed at eleven o'clock on 11 November 1918, but despite this and the fact that there was no longer the same need for munitions, the committee and players of Dick, Kerr Ladies decided to carry on as far as possible with their fixtures. After all, the local charities were in as great a need of help as ever they had been before.

An interesting article appeared in the *Lancashire Daily Post* on 15 November 1919 holding that women were unsuitable to act as referees. Journalist John Lewis said,

> As far as I am aware there is nothing in the rules to stop a woman officiating as a referee, but it would not be an enviable position for her to occupy in serious football at all events. For one thing, a woman could not reasonably be expected to keep pace with men and could hardly follow the game as we expect a man to do. It would be an innovation to have a woman in charge of a match. From my own experience I am certain she would discover that refereeing an exciting match is nothing like as easy as it may seem to some spectators. I have not heard of a female umpire in League or County Cricket, or that a woman has ever had charge of a boxing contest. I have no objections whatever to the fair sex participating in sports, but at the same time they are not suitable candidates for the position of referee, which post they would find neither very pleasant nor happy, especially if trouble arose with players or onlookers. In a word, the duty cannot be successfully discharged by a woman though if they qualify there is nothing as far as I am aware to prevent their being recognised by the referees' associations.

The first peacetime match played by Dick, Kerr Ladies took place at Deepdale on 23 November 1918. Their opponents were from the British Westinghouse works, Manchester. The Manchester side were no match for the home team, who had a comfortable 4–0 win. Once again, Kell and Redford stole the headlines and were the star players.

It was obvious that the need for charity was on the increase. Wounded and disabled soldiers and sailors, wives, mothers and children whose husbands, sons or fathers did not return from war-torn Europe, were all in need of help as they tried to come to terms with life without their loved ones.

Dick, Kerr Ladies set about their task in earnest and a busy fund-raising December lay ahead. They played Lancaster Ladies at Deepdale on 21 December and suffered the second defeat of their career, going down 1–0. Lancaster had the two best players on the field in Jennie Harris and Jessie Walmsley, and their goalkeeper Annie Hastie gave a good account of herself. If Nellie Mitchell and Elsie Arnold had taken the easiest of chances in the second half, however, Dick, Kerr's could have won the game.

Following their defeat, the management committee of the club wasted no time, strengthening the side in time for their Christmas Day fixture with Bolton Ladies. Four days after helping Lancaster to victory over Dick, Kerr Ladies, Annie Hastie and Jennie Harris, the goalkeeper and centre-forward, were in the line-up with the Preston side.

Eight thousand people went to Deepdale on Christmas Day 1918, and witnessed a thrilling game between Dick, Kerr's and Bolton Ladies, which resulted in a 2–2 draw. The result represented the merits of both sides and although the pitch was on the heavy side, the game was played at a remarkable pace. Bolton took the lead through Florrie Haslam who, after receiving the ball in her own half, outpaced all the opposition to score a fine goal. Molly Walker equalized for Dick, Kerr's just before half time. After the interval, M. Gibbons put Bolton in the lead, but Nellie Mitchell made it 2–2 after converting a centre from Molly Walker. The receipts, which totalled about £180, were divided among local charities.

In their first game of the new year, on 10 January 1919, against another Bolton team, the ladies had yet another Lancaster player in their line-up in Jessie Walmsley, their centre-half. They now had four players in their side who had originally started with Lancaster Ladies, Molly Walker being the first.

What was it that convinced these women to move from Lancaster to Preston? As far as football was concerned, Lancaster were a good team in their own right. In their last three meetings with Dick, Kerr Ladies they had won one, drawn one, and lost one, and they were the only team to inflict a defeat upon Whitehaven Ladies in the previous two seasons. Perhaps the promise of a job at the factory was the deciding factor. And what was in it for Dick, Kerr & Co. Ltd? Could it really be that their only motives were of a sporting nature? Or were there other reasons for their accommodating the women at the factory?

Dick, Kerr Ladies' aim to be the best was being realized and they were now recognized as the strongest side in the country. In their next match at Deepdale, on 25 January 1919, their opponents were Heywood Ladies, a team that included several of the Bolton side. They had been asked to get as strong an eleven as possible from the area, so that they could provide better opposition.

Women's football was becoming increasingly popular, and so teams were travelling further afield in order to meet fresh and stronger opposition. On 8 March 1919, Dick, Kerr Ladies played Newcastle United Ladies at Deepdale in their last home match of the season. The Newcastle side, who had travelled overnight to play the fixture, had built up a good reputation for their goalscoring ability; one of their forwards, W. McKenna, had already scored over 130 goals before the game with Dick, Kerr's. For this match, Dick, Kerr's strengthened their side with the inclusion of three members of the Bolton team: Rawsthorne, Hulme and Partington. The match ended in a 1–0 win for the home team, the goal scored by Nellie Mitchell. The return match at St James's Park, Newcastle was played in front of 35,000 people. The Preston team included their new signing, Florrie Haslam from Bolton Ladies, who came the closest to scoring in the 0–0 draw.

Another major signing for Dick, Kerr's in 1919 was Alice Woods from St Helens. Alice was already a top-class sprinter and she was the first woman to win a race held under AAA laws. The race, run over eighty yards, was held at Blackpool in 1918. She could run 100 yards in twelve seconds.

She began playing football while working in a munitions factory at St Helens, but her mother was not happy about it. Alice told her brother Jack, who played centre-forward for Halifax Town, that she had been asked to join the factory team but knew her mother would not really like it. Jack said to Alice, 'There's no

Dick, Kerr's at New Brighton, 1919.

need for Mum to know,' and he taught her how to play the game. He showed her on a blackboard what the positions were and taught her how to head, kick, trap and dribble with the ball. Her natural speed was always an asset.

After playing in a match for St Helens against Dick, Kerr's, and scoring a goal for her team, she was approached by Mr Frankland and asked if she would like to play for Dick, Kerr Ladies. She declined at first, but following a further visit to her home by a characteristically determined Mr Frankland, she agreed to the transfer. She went to stay at the home of Alice Kell when she moved to Preston.

Lydia Ackers was another St Helens player to make the move to Preston. She played for the St Helens team until its disbandment; she recalls, 'That's when they came to my home because they must have heard about me.' Her mother felt Lydia was too young to leave home and did not really want her to go away. Mr Frankland, however, assured her that her daughter would be well looked after because they wanted them all together at the factory in Preston. Lydia remembers, 'They eventually got us all together and they found us "digs". I had a very good place in Avenham. The first thing I can remember was the "knocker-up" knocking at the window. I came from the countryside and it was something I had never heard of before.' (The 'knocker-up' was a man whose job it was to extinguish the gas lamps in the streets at first light. With the long pole needed to snuff out the lamps he could also knock on upstairs bedroom windows to waken people who worked on early shifts, and he would do this to earn an extra few shillings every week.)

Alice Norris was a local girl who started work at Dick, Kerr's in 1919 when she was fourteen years old. Born in Preston in 1905, she was employed at the company until she retired in 1965. Alice remembers playing football with the apprentices at the back of the works. 'We used to play at shooting at the cloakroom windows. They were little square windows and if the boys beat us at putting a window through we had to buy them a packet of Woodbines, but if we beat them they had to buy us a bar of "five boys" chocolate.'

Alice was spotted playing football by one of the men connected with the ladies' team and he asked her father if she could play for them. Alice and her father went up to see Mr Frankland and she was allowed to play for the team on condition that it did not interfere with the family.

Alice says, 'There was a good friendly spirit at the club; you didn't hear anyone arguing with one another, and it was a privilege to play for them. The older players would always take care of the younger ones and I remember Florrie Redford was very good to me. When we played on First Division grounds she used to look after me. After the game there would usually be a reception for us and there would be tables set up with our team on one side, Mr Frankland and all the officials across the top, and the other team down the other side. On one occasion there was this man who had taken quite a shine to me and he was really annoying me. Flo came across and told him to leave me alone. When he told her it was none of her business she told him, in no uncertain terms, that I was her younger sister and it was very much her business. It just showed how the older ones like Flo Redford and Alice Kell would keep an eye on you to make sure you were all right. It was like being part of a big family.'

There was obviously a good atmosphere at the club, with great camaraderie between the girls, and success followed success. By the end of 1919 they were well and truly established as *the* team to beat, and the next few years would see them achieve more than they could ever have dared to dream of.

The 1920s saw the team lose the first match of the new decade to Liverpool Ladies, on 7 February, by 2–0. They then suffered a further defeat at the hands of Liverpool, losing 1–0 at Wigan on 10 April. Out of thirty matches played during 1920, however, they were to lose only one more game.

Perhaps the most significant find of Dick, Kerr Ladies Football Club was that of fourteen-year-old Lily Parr. In her first season with the club (1919/20), she scored an amazing total of forty-three goals. Lily had lived in St Helens and she came to Preston on the recommendation of Alice Woods. Alice must have told Alfred Frankland of Lily's footballing ability, and following her signing for Dick, Kerr Ladies, she was taken in at the home of Alice Norris, whose mother agreed to let Lily stay at their home on the understanding that she would share a room with Alice.

Alice recalls, 'I had two sisters and we all lived in a three-bedroomed house, so there was enough room to take her in, but when Lily came to stay and we went upstairs to show her the bedroom we were supposed to be sharing, she threw me out and my nightclothes came out after me! I never got back in my room much after that, not while Lily was staying with us anyway.'

Lily Parr was born on 26 April 1905, and it has to be said that she was way ahead of her time. The old saying of the mould being broken when someone was born was certainly true of Lily; she was, without doubt, a 'one-off'. A dominant footballing figure, she was to continue playing the game she loved until 1951, and probably the greatest woman footballer of all time. Yet she was an extremely shy person, and with strangers she found it very difficult to speak in public. When all the speeches and thank-yous were being exchanged at post-match receptions, Lily could only ever manage to speak one sentence in front of a room full of people, much preferring to let her feet do the talking.

Standing almost six feet tall, with jet-black hair, her power and skill were admired and feared wherever she played. She was an extremely unselfish player who could pass with amazing accuracy and also had marvellous ball control. She was probably responsible, in one way or another, for most of the goals scored by the team. Once, while playing a game at Chorley, in Lancashire, she was challenged by a professional male goalkeeper to try to put the ball past him while he stood in goal. It was his chauvinistic opinion, after watching Lily 'shooting in', that her capabilities and power of shot might have looked impressive against other women but would certainly be no match for a man. Never one to shirk a challenge, Lily took a shot at the male goalkeeper and, as he put his hands up to catch the ball, his arm was broken by the force of her kick. Lily smiled to herself as she heard him say to his team-mates, 'Bloody hell, get me to the hospital as quick as you can, she's broken me bloody arm.'

Something of an enigmatic figure, Lily was the original 'rough diamond' with a heart of gold. She didn't worry about authority, rules or regulations, she was very much her own person, and if she wanted to do something, she would simply do it. Her manner was described as rough, somewhat brusque on the outside but soft on the inside; coming from the poorer end of St Helens, she had had to be strong to survive. There was little work about in her home town at the time, so a move to Preston to work and play football was a golden opportunity for her. Alice Norris says of the teenaged Lily Parr, 'She had an enormous appetite; I'm sure my mother must have been out of pocket with her, she could eat for England!'

Alice continues: 'What I found strange, though, was that during all the time that Lily stayed with us, I never once heard her speak about her family. When we all played football with the apprentices, we used to club together to buy a 6d ball from Woolworth's. One particular time, my two younger sisters, who had been quite poorly, were going to stay at a convalescent home in Lytham, near Blackpool, and I thought it would be a good idea for them to take one of these balls with them so that they would have something to play with. In those days we didn't have anywhere near as many toys as children have today, and to us things were precious. So, as I was working overtime I asked Lily if she would take the ball home and give it to my father for the girls to take with them while they were convalescing in Lytham. When I got home from work and asked him if Lily had given him the ball, he said that she had and he had bought it from her for 6d. I said, "You what! She sold it to you! But I got that ball for them." "Well," said Father, "I paid her 6d for it, just like she asked." But that was Lily, you never knew what she was going to do next.'

Lily was a deep-voiced, yet quietly-spoken woman with a droll sense of humour, who often had people in fits of laughter at her wry comments. Joan Whalley tells of Lily's dressing-room banter, saying, 'When the older players were getting ready for a match, there would be elastic stockings going on knees and the strapping up of ankles, there were bandages here there and everywhere. Then Parr walked in [they often referred to one another by their surnames] and she stood looking around at them all and said, "Well, I don't know about Dick, Kerr Ladies football team, it looks like a bloody trip to Lourdes to me!"

'The team once went along to be photographed on Ashton Park and we all got changed in a big old house. There was nothing in the place, it was completely empty. After the photographs had been taken and we went back in, Parr said to me, "Come here Whalley" (she never called me Joan, all my life it was always Whalley). I knew she had something up her sleeve because she used to get me doing all her jobs for her, I was only young. "Come with me, Whalley, I've something to show you." I went following along at her heels like a little puppy. She went into a room where there was an old sideboard, it was nearly falling to bits. She opened a drawer and there were all sorts of knives and forks in it. She said to me, "Do you think they're silver?" "Of course they are," I replied, "they've got silver stamped on them." She asked me to help her get some of them, but I told her I didn't want to get involved. "Get hold of them," she said, "there's nobody wants them, they wouldn't be left lying around here if they did. I could make use of these, and with a bit of cleaning up they'd be lovely on the table. Come on Whalley, get hold of them." "No," I said, "I'm not pinching for you," and I left her to it.

'Wherever she went she used to try and take the football from the games. We always autographed the match ball and it would be raffled off to raise more money for charity. The game would be kicked off by some well-known celebrity with the ball that we had all signed, then we would play the game with another new ball. After the match someone would always come looking for the football. "Where's the match ball, where's the ball?" But it was nearly always missing. I would say to some of the others, "It'll be that Parr again." She would be looking in all the corners, pretending to be looking for it, and we would be daft enough to help look for it as well. How many balls she got away with I don't know, but she would produce them on the bus when we were miles away from the venue. We never knew what she did with them all, we suspected that she must have sold them.'

After leaving the employ of Dick, Kerr & Co. Ltd, like many of the other players, Lily Parr began a career as a nurse at Whittingham Hospital, just outside Preston, where she was to stay until her retirement in the 1960s. There, too, Lily was not afraid of breaking the rules. In those days, the matron was a fearsome woman who had most lesser mortals shaking in their shoes. Lily always loved a smoke and she often held her cigarette with her hand cupped around it. Smoking on the wards was considered a mortal sin and definitely not allowed. But if Lily needed a quick intake of nicotine, she would not hesitate to light up whenever the urge took her. It had been known for her to be seen talking to the matron with her hand cupped behind her back with a lighted cigarette in it!

She was a good nurse, though, kind and caring, and although they were not supposed to have favourites, Lily often did. One particular old lady, Kitty, of whom Lily had grown fond, had passed away. Lily was quite upset and could not help shedding a few tears for the old girl. But of course she would never admit to anyone that she had been crying and she passed off her sniffles as 'having a bad cold'.

On another occasion, she came across an ex-patient while out shopping. She enquired after the lady's health and asked how things were. The lady confided to Lily that she had fallen on hard times and was about to have her electricity supply cut off as she was unable to pay the bill. Without any hesitation, Lily asked how much it was and gave her the money to pay for it. Such was her

Lily Parr (far right), who played for Dick, Kerr's from 1919 to 1951, seen here having a joke with a French player in the late 1940s.

much it was and gave her the money to pay for it. Such was her kindness and generosity.

A year or two into her retirement, Lily noticed a lump in her breast which resulted in her needing to have a mastectomy. Five or six weeks later, she found another lump in her other breast and had to undergo a second mastectomy. She retained her sense of humour throughout her ordeal, however, and was brave about her illness. Referring to her operations, Lily would joke, 'It's taken me sixty-two years to grow these, now they've taken the bloody things off me!'

A friend visiting Lily in hospital after her double mastectomy was unsure what gift to take for her, as she knew that she had already received several floral bouquets. Her friend knew that Lily was not particularly fond of flowers, so she decided to take what she knew Lily would appreciate the most: a packet of Woodbines!

'Thank God for some bloody cigs,' said Lily, 'I can't get hold of any in here, they won't let me have them.'

Lily lived for ten years after her second operation, but was finally beaten by cancer and died at her home in Goosnargh, near Preston, on 24 May 1978, and then this special lady was finally laid to rest in her native St Helens.

Without question, Lily Parr was one of the most influential and charismatic women ever to wear the famous colours of Dick, Kerr Ladies Football Club. Those whose lives she touched were a little richer for having known her.

2 Playing the French Home and Away

By 1920, women's football was becoming accepted as a spectator sport, rather than as a novelty, as most men would apparently prefer to believe. More and more charitable organizations were recognizing this fact by placing considerable demands on the ladies to play more matches up and down the country.

In France, too, women had begun to play football after the war, and although not as experienced as their British counterparts, they were none the less quick and skilful.

It seemed to the management of Dick, Kerr Ladies that the next step in the evolution of the women's game would be to invite a team from France over to England to play football, for obvious charitable reasons. The defence of French soil by British soldiers during the recent war had set up strong ties between the two nations, and what better way for France to give something back than to send a women's football team to England to play for British charities?

Ever the ones to forge ahead and break new ground, Dick, Kerr Ladies had contacted the Fédération des Sociétés Feminines Sportives de France, and invited a French representative team to play a series of matches in England in aid of the National Association of Discharged and Disabled Soldiers and Sailors. The invitation was accepted and four matches were arranged to be played at Preston, Stockport, Manchester and Chelsea. Mr Frankland travelled to Dover to welcome the French team to England and accompanied them to London.

After their long journey, which included a rough Channel crossing, the girls looked pale, cold and tired when they descended from the continental train at Victoria Station, London, but they quickly brightened up with the warm welcome given to them by a host of pressmen and others. This was the first time any of the

24

girls had been in England and Madame Milliat, their trainer, said, 'We are very happy to be here and we are looking forward to a most pleasant visit. Of course, the girls are all very excited and full of it.' The party consisted of seventeen players, whose ages ranged between eighteen and twenty-five years: Mlle Duray (shop assistant and interpreter), Mlles Laloz (sisters – machine workers), Mlle Rigal (dressmaker), Mlle Pomies (dental student), Mlles Rinbaux, Brule, and Bracquemond (shorthand typists), Mlle Delpierre (student of philosophy), Mlle Billac (bookkeeper), Mlle Patuneau (dressmaker), Mlles Trotmann (sisters, English-speaking, whose mother came from Leeds) and Mlles Janiaud, Viani and Ourry. Mdme Leveque was the only married player in the team.

They arrived at Preston on Wednesday 28 April 1920, shortly after 6 p.m. As the train pulled into the station, the Dick, Kerr's prize band greeted the French football team with the 'Marseillaise', and members of their club cheered loudly. As they stepped off the train one of the players was waving a toy rabbit which they had brought as the team's mascot. A big crowd closed in around them, and an army of press photographers struggled to photograph the ladies before the officials of Dick, Kerr Ladies were introduced and greetings exchanged. A bouquet of flowers was presented to Madame Milliat.

They were obviously surprised and visibly moved by the warmth of Preston's welcome, but very happy because of it, and they all had one of the most enjoyable experiences of their lives. A huge crowd had gathered at the station approach and thousands had lined up in Fishergate to give an enthusiastic welcome to the French visitors. The Dick, Kerr's band led the way up Fishergate, followed by the French team, who were driven up to their hotel in a wagonette draped with the French tricolour and drawn by four light bay horses. Their faces beamed with delight at the wonderful reception given them by the crowds. At the rear of the procession was a motor charabanc (open coach) containing the Dick, Kerr players and officials.

The Bull and Royal Hotel, where the team stayed throughout their visit, was decorated with streamers of allied flags for the occasion. One P.C. Tomlinson, a policemen on duty outside the hotel, was able to speak fluently in French with the visitors; during the war, he had acted as an interpreter with British forces in France.

The team was representative of ladies' football teams in Paris, where the federation controlled women's and girls' athletics.

The French team, 1920.

Madame Milliat was the founder of the federation and her knowledge and experience of association football was probably unequalled by that of any other woman in France. She is quoted in a newpaper article in Mr Frankland's scrapbook as saying, 'In my opinion, football is not wrong for women. Most of these girls are beautiful Grecian dancers. I do not think it is unwomanly to play football as they do not play like men, they play fast, but not vigorous football.'

The French girls were mainly on the small side, but most of them were all-round athletes and they hoped, by their superior speed, to make a good fight of it in the coming matches with Dick, Kerr Ladies.

After dinner at the hotel the party were driven to the canteen at the Dick, Kerr works, where a dance had been arranged for their entertainment. At the dance, Madame Milliat expressed herself as deeply touched by the remarkable reception given to them upon their arrival in the town. A full programme of entertainment was arranged for them during their ten-day visit. A visit to Horrockses, a local cotton mill, and a charabanc trip to Whalley was arranged for Thursday 29 April, and on the Friday they visited the Dick, Kerr works, where they saw the manufacture of all kinds of electrical machinery, electric lamps and tram cars in progress. At the lamp works, a glass loving cup made on the premises was presented to the team. In the evening they left the hotel by charabanc, preceded by the Preston Military Band, en route to Deepdale for their first match against the host team. At the ground, the Dick, Kerr band played selections before the start of the game, 'Rule Britannia' and the 'Marseillaise' being among them.

A crowd of 25,000 came to Deepdale to watch the opening match of the ladies' tour. Dick, Kerr's lined up in their now famous black-and-white stripes, and the French team played in light blue jerseys with a red, white and blue cockade on the left breast, and navy-blue shorts. The French girls were beaten by 2–0 with goals scored by Florrie Redford and Jennie Harris.*

Dick, Kerr's almost ran the French defence to a standstill with their superior play, but for all their possession, they were still unable to score more than two goals. The outstanding feature of the game was the work of Jennie Harris at inside-left, Florrie Redford at inside-right and Alice Kell, the captain and right back.

---

* All match reports and quotes are taken from undated press clippings in Mr Frankland's scrapbook.

No player on either side reached anything near the high standard of play these three players set in the game. Jessie Walmsley in defence broke up the French attacks well, while Molly Walker twisted her knee early in the game and had to come off just after half time. Lily Lee also hurt her knee and played with some difficulty during the second half. For the French team, Carmen Pomies, one of the sturdiest players on view, gave a good performance ably assisted by Viani. Alice Trotmann and Bracquemond were the pick of their attack, while Ourry, an alert and competent goalkeeper, frequently gained applause from the crowd.

At the end of the match, Jennie Harris, who was quickly taken to the heart of the crowd thanks to her skilful play, was carried shoulder-high off the field by spectators who had swarmed on to the pitch. Madame Milliat said afterwards that she had never seen such a big crowd at a match, commenting that they did not get crowds of that size at men's matches in Paris. Indeed, it must be said that seldom had a bigger crowd been seen at Deepdale's famous enclosure.

Saturday saw both teams travel by charabanc to Stockport, where they were met at Mersey Square and taken to the ground for the evening match. The crowd saw an emphatic victory for the Dick, Kerr team with a 5–2 defeat for the French ladies, who must have been very tired after their full schedule.

On Sunday, the visitors were entertained at the home of Mr Frankland, and Monday saw them on a charabanc visit to a very breezy Blackpool. Tuesday, they had the day to themselves to rest and prepare for their next match.

The game at Hyde Road, Manchester, on Wednesday, in front of 12,000 spectators, was a well-deserved 1–1 draw between Dick, Kerr's and the French ladies. Obviously benefiting from their day of rest, the French girls played well, especially in attack, and had it not been for the excellent work of Dick, Kerr's goalkeeper, they would have added at least two more goals. So delighted was one of the French players at her team scoring that she did a complete somersault and landed on her feet. On the other hand, the Preston girls played some good football and were unlucky on several occasions in front of goal.

Madame Milliat was presented with a manicure set by the National Association of Discharged Soldiers and Sailors in recognition of the fact that the proceeds of all the matches were in aid of the ex-servicemen's fund. The gross receipts for the match amounted to £766 11s 5d. The two previous matches at Preston and Stockport had raised some £2,000.

The final match of the tour was played at Stamford Bridge, the home of Chelsea Football Club. A crowd of 10,000 saw the French ladies record their first victory against the Dick, Kerr team, by 2–1. Jennie Harris, the Preston inside-left, was knocked out early in the game, which reduced the Lancashire team to ten players.

Brule, the French full-back, was in good form as was Alice Kell, the Dick, Kerr Ladies captain. The crowd thoroughly enjoyed the game. 'I never thought girls could play till full time,' was one spectator's view. 'Nor kick so hard,' added another. A quaint French touch was given to the victory when Alice Kell was kissed by Bracquemond, and she threw her arms around her opponent's shoulder as they walked off the field together.

So as the tour came to a close, both teams could be satisfied at a job well done. They had played their part in raising over £3,000 for worthwhile charities, and the French ladies had recorded a famous victory over a team recognized as the best in the land.

During their ten-day visit, thousands of people had turned out to wish them well. Many friends were made both on and off the field and the whole tour was without doubt a resounding success. Addresses were exchanged between the teams, and a promise to 'keep in touch' was warmly made. It was hoped that a return visit to France could be made by Dick, Kerr's team sometime in the autumn.

Upon their return to Paris, the French team were given a warm welcome. Parents, friends and representatives of the girls' athletic societies were at the Gare du Nord to present the ladies with so many bouquets that there were several for each player. A railway porter, moved by the reception given to the ladies, was heard to shout, '*Vive la France!*'

The girls' description of their stay in England was uniformly enthusiastic. Madame Milliat said that the success of the tour had far exceeded their expectations: 'We were simply overpowered with kindness, and we must give the English girls a welcome worthy of them when they come here in the autumn.' When asked if they had enjoyed themselves, they replied, 'Why yes, but we found it very windy on Blackpool front.'

Ourry, the French goalkeeper, returned to Preston shortly after the tour, to play for Dick, Kerr Ladies. She received valuable coaching from them, and her goalkeeping ability was certainly improved because of it.

Two days after the French ladies returned home to Paris, Dick, Kerr's were back on the victory trail. On Saturday, 8 May, a crowd of 15,000 came to Oldham to see them defeat St Helens Ladies by 2–0.

A busy spring and summer lay ahead, which saw them undefeated as they travelled throughout Lancashire, Cheshire and into Yorkshire. With the exception of the month of July, they played a match almost every Saturday throughout this period.

A day trip to Blackpool at holiday times was undoubtedly considered an adventure in those days, yet here was a group of ordinary working-class girls taking the country by storm. It is easy to forget just what a woman's standing was at this point in history. The suffragettes had fought and died for women to have the right to vote, a fight which had only recently been won at the general election of December 1918, when women over thirty were allowed to vote for the first time. Travelling up and down the land playing football, with civic receptions held in their honour, admired and respected wherever they went, Dick, Kerr Ladies must have considered themselves to be the emancipated women of the 1920s.

The final arrangements were under way for the return visit to France, and the girls were undergoing intensive training as part of their preparations for the tour. They were fortunate to have had some excellent coaching from many famous footballers who had been, or still were, working at the Strand Road works. Bob Holmes, the famous old North End 'Invincible'; Johnny Morley, Burnley and North End; Billy Grier, North End centre-half and Jack Warner the North End and Portsmouth full-back, had all given them the benefit of their skill and experience.

Mr Birkenshaw, their trainer, was an enthusiastic man who always put the girls through their paces, and training was as strict and thorough as it would have been with any First Division league club. The girls kept themselves fit by sprinting, skipping and ball practice, and they felt that no other ladies' team could be in better condition.

They were also fortunate in having the use of their own training ground. Dick, Kerr & Co. Ltd had bought Ashton Park at the beginning of 1920. The eighty-three-acre site was used as a sports and recreation ground for the company's employees. It had a cricket pitch, a nine-hole golf course, tennis courts and a football pitch. There was a mansion house on the park and it was said to have a memorial on a wall with the names of all the company's workers who had lost their lives during the war.

The football pitch was situated at the corner of Blackpool Road and Pedders Lane, and it was surrounded by wooden hoardings, making it a private enclosure. It was known locally as 'Lively Polly Corner', so called because Lively Polly was the name of a washing powder, and posters advertising the product were pasted all around the pitch on the hoardings.

The team were all looking forward to the trip to France and Alice Kell, the captain, said,

> We intend showing the people of France what fine sportswomen the English women are, and we shall not allow sentiment to creep in quite as much as we did when the French team played over here earlier this year. Of course we didn't underestimate them, or allow them to win, but we didn't put in the 'last ounce' as you might say. And we were unlucky at having more than our fair share of injuries to our players in all the matches with the French ladies. Surely we will not have the same bad luck again.*

Alice had always loved playing football, since she was a little girl. Her brothers were keen footballers, and many a tough game was had with them on Preston marsh. Alice lived on Marsh Lane and went to the Hincksman Memorial School, Croft Street, where she and her best friend Florrie Redford had been inseparable. Both girls later worked together at Dick, Kerr & Co. Ltd, and they jumped at the chance of playing football in a women's team.

The night before their departure to France the team and their friends were entertained to dinner and a musical evening at the works canteen, attended by the Mayor and Mayoress, Alderman and Mrs T. Parkinson.

Mr R. Livingstone, works manager, presided at the concert, and in wishing the team success on the trip, paid tribute to its good work since its formation in 1917. He said that the firm had expanded and was now one of the largest companies in the world, with branches in Australia, France and Japan. He hoped that in the not too distant future, in addition to the team's present tour, they would try to go to some of these other countries. In addition

---

* Untitled newspaper article in Mr Frankland's scrapbook

Mr Adlington, chairman of the club, spoke of the team's splendid work for charity and said that £8,600 had been raised, mainly for local charities, since the club's inception.

Mr Frankland, also speaking of the team's success and in thanking the firm for their kindness to them, said that they hoped to uphold the traditions of the town and the firm on the tour, on which they hoped to win all four matches.

Alice Kell said, 'If the matches with the French ladies serve no other purpose, I feel that they will have done more to cement the good feeling between the two nations than anything which has occurred during the last fifty years, except of course the Great War.'

Some of the players had lost brothers in the war and they hoped to be able to place wreaths on the public memorials to British soldiers in the four towns where their matches were to be played. It was also hoped they could place a wreath, tied with the colours of Blackburn Rovers, on the grave of Eddie Latheron, the Ewood club's international inside-right, who was killed while serving with the Royal Field Artillery at Passchendaele. The tour was also to take in visits to battlefields in the Ypres Salient.

Those making the historic trip, thus becoming the first British women's football club to embark on an overseas football tour, were: Alfred Frankland, secretary; A. E. Howarth, treasurer; and E. Birkenshaw, trainer. The sixteen players were: Alice Kell, Annie Hastie, Lily Parr, Alice Woods, Jessie Walmsley, Sally Hulme, Florrie Haslam, Minnie Lyons, Daisy Clayton, Emily Jones, Lily Jones, Florrie Redford, Jennie Harris, Molly Walker, Lily Lee and Annie Crozier. Lily Jones was to be married in London on the return journey.

Letters had been regularly sent between the two teams since the French visit to England and the Preston girls were busy brushing up on their French in readiness for the tour.

On Thursday 28 October 1920, Dick, Kerr Ladies left Preston for London en route for Paris. The streets were lined with cheering crowds as they were driven up to the railway station in a motor charabanc decorated with the Union Jack and the French tricolour. A big crowd had also gathered at the station approach to see them safely on their way, and a huge cheer went up as Alice Kell waved the club's mascot, a teddy bear dressed in a Union Jack, from the train as it pulled out of the station.

They arrived in London at 5.30 p.m. and made their way to the Bonnington Hotel for dinner and an overnight stay. They took

Leaving for France, November 1920.
Left to right: Jennie Harris, Alice Kell, Annie Hastie, Florrie Haslam, Flo Redford, Daisy Clayton, Jessie Walmsley, Molly Walker, Alice Woods, Lily Parr, Lily Lee (the rest unknown).

the opportunity while in the capital to visit the Palladium, returning to their hotel at midnight.

The next morning, Friday, they left London at eleven o'clock and arrived in Dover mid-afternoon, where they met an old Prestonian, Billy Maile, now a customs official. He was an old schoolfriend of Florrie Redford and Alice Kell, and he was so delighted at meeting his old friends, and the rest of the Dick, Kerr team, that he travelled across to Calais with them. The Channel crossing was not the smoothest of journeys and only five of the party showed they had 'sea legs' and escaped the sickness, but this was soon overcome when they landed on French soil.

Travelling by train from Calais to Paris, they passed by Etaples cemetery, where many British soldiers were buried. Mr Frankland expressed the hope that it would be of some consolation to many British mothers to know that the cemetery was beautifully kept and full of flowers.

They were met by Mrs Trotmann, an English lady from Leeds, whose daughters had been on the French team's tour of England. Mrs Trotmann soon took control of the team, and she said that out of twenty-three years of French life, this was the happiest time she had ever had. She travelled with the team on the tour, acting as guide and interpreter.

They reached Paris at 7.30 p.m. and were met by the French team, who broke past the police at the Gare du Nord in their anxiety to greet the Preston team as soon as the train arrived. They presented Alice Kell with a beautiful bouquet of flowers. Cheer after cheer rang out and the party began singing 'She's a Lassie from Lancashire'. On leaving the station the Dick, Kerr team were amused at seeing French policemen carrying long sabres and their uniform reminded them of gas inspectors at home in Preston.

They were all tired and hungry after their long journey and so they were relieved when they arrived at the Hotel Beau Séjour, where they freshened up before having dinner. Although none of them was particularly fond of French cuisine, they all did full justice to their evening meal.

On Saturday 30 October, they were taken on a trip around Paris. They saw all the sights, drove along the Champs Elysées and climbed to the top of the Arc de Triomphe, up 281 steps. Next stop on the sightseeing tour was Notre Dame, and they saw the spot where Napoleon was married to Josephine in 1804. They were also shown the windows, which contain something like 300,000 pieces of glass. The windows had to be taken out during 'Big

Bertha's bombardment of Paris during the war. (Big Bertha was a huge German gun, transported on railway lines. The gun shelled Paris from the Forest of Coucy, seventy-six miles away.)

There were many British soldiers in Paris still on active service, and they greeted the team warmly. Both they and the French people were seeking autographs and wanting to be photographed with the team. Everyone in Paris seemed to want to see the match at the Pershing Stadium the next day.

When they returned to the hotel for lunch, they were hoping for something more familiar to eat than what they had tasted so far, so a loud cheer went up among them when they were served with steak and chips. After lunch, with thoughts of home never far away, the girls were asking if there would be any means of getting to know in the evening how North End had gone on that afternoon. They were missing their *Football Post*!

On Sunday 31 October the team spent the morning doing more sightseeing. They left their hotel at 9.30 a.m. for the French Military Training School, where they were treated to lunch and then entertained by Colonel Seé and his officers. They were shown an exhibition of slow photography of all the famous French athletes performing, a special feature in the French Army that showed the men the correct way of executing movements. Georges Carpentier, the boxer, was an instructor there during the war, and Colonel Seé told Mr Frankland that Carpentier had been one of his best pupils. Afterwards, they were asked to sign an autograph book, kept for all the champion French athletes to sign their names in. All the girls signed their names and Mr Frankland added in the book, 'Dick, Kerr Ladies Football Club desire to place on record their grateful appreciation of the splendid manner in which they have been received by the Officers of our Brave French Allies. Long Live France!' Following their visit to the military training school, they walked across to the Pershing Stadium to prepare for the opening match of the tour.

Twenty-two thousand people came to the stadium to see the two sides play to a 1–1 draw. Both goals were scored in the first half. The French Air Minister kicked off, and at the start the Dick, Kerr team seemed rather nervous, but they soon settled down and kept the French team hemmed in their own half for the first twenty-five minutes. A breakaway goal was then scored by Laloz, whose superior speed saw her find the Dick, Kerr net. This spurred on the Preston side, who had shot after shot at the French goal, only to find Ourry playing as well as she had while with their team in England. Minnie Lyons had a good shot from thirty yards out, however, which gave Ourry no chance. There was a big cheer from the Englishmen in the crowd, who obviously knew the team well. They were heard to shout, 'Play up Dick, Kerr's', and 'Play up Lancashire'. The French team were lucky to be on level terms at half time.

The scores remained the same throughout the second half, when the game ended in a most sensational manner. The French referee awarded a corner kick to Dick, Kerr's with only five minutes of the match remaining. This was met with protests from a large section of the French spectators, who immediately invaded the pitch. Players from both teams were surrounded by the crowd and so the referee abandoned the game with four minutes still to play. The players were escorted away safely, however, as the crowd were in good humour, and there was no trouble at all. After the game, Alice Kell said that the French ladies were much better on their home ground; they had improved since their visit to England.

Playing football on a Sunday seemed strange to the Preston team, as Sunday in England was regarded as the Sabbath. Mr Frankland said of it, 'After our experience, we say the English Sunday is something to be proud of. In Paris, the fairground was open, it was like our Whitsuntide fairs, and the market halls and theatres were open. One wonders when the French get their rest.'

The next morning they left Paris at half past six for Roubaix, and on the journey they passed through some of the more devastated regions, seeing at first hand evidence of war-torn France. They saw the trenches still full of water, shell hobs and barbed-wire entanglements, they saw people rebuilding homes reduced to ruins by the bombs, living in small huts made out of oil drums picked up from the dumps. Mr Frankland said that people who had not seen these parts could never conceive what northern France must have suffered and endured, but that rebuilding was going on at a fast pace.

The match in Roubaix kicked off at 3.15 p.m. in front of 16,000 spectators, a record for this ground, doubling all past records. The French team were given a tremendous ovation on coming out on to the field, but the reception given to Dick, Kerr's from the British spectators was like a cup final. Dick, Kerr Ladies probably played the best football of their lives, and during the first half the French did not get a look in. They could hear the crowd shouting 'Good old Dick, Kerr's', and 'Play up Proud Preston'. They could almost have been playing at Deepdale. Alice Kell, Florrie Redford, Jennie Harris and Florrie Haslam all played great football, but there were no goals scored in the first half.

After the interval, Dick, Kerr's carried on where they had left off. Florrie Redford opened the scoring with a well-taken goal and the crowd went wild. Union Jacks and black-and-white colours were waved all over the ground. Then, with ten minutes to go, Dick, Kerr's were awarded a penalty. Redford took the kick and scored with a great shot just wide of the left hand of the goalkeeper. The game throughout was played at a fast pace and Dick, Kerr's were always on top, the 2–0 scoreline not doing the quality of their play full justice. At the end of the match the whole team were carried shoulder-high off the field by the British spectators, delighted with the English victory.

Later, on arrival at their hotel, they were given the most wonderful reception from a crowd of about 250 British soldiers and Lancashire workmen, the latter there to help with the French rebuilding programme. They had gathered outside the hotel to welcome the victorious team. They also discovered that about sixty-five Englishmen were staying in the hotel itself. They had come from all parts of northern France to get a glimpse of the players. Mr Frankland said in the *Lancashire Daily Post*, 'Words fail to describe how glad they all were to see our team, I cannot describe their hearty greetings, I have never seen a team get a better reception than ours did.'

On Tuesday, the company of Dick, Kerr Ladies Football Club went to pay their respects and lay a wreath at the cenotaph in Roubaix, for all the soldiers who had given their lives during the war. Alice Kell was helped to place the wreath, which was twelve feet in diameter, at the foot of the memorial. It was a poignant reminder of why they had all begun playing football during the Great War in 1917.

The rest of the week was taken up with sightseeing. Wednesday they went to the top of the Eiffel Tower and to the circus. On Thursday, they were up at 6.30 a.m. for a trip to Versailles, where they were given a guided tour of the royal palace. They saw the table at which the peace treaty had been signed on Armistice Day, and they also went through the famous Hall of Mirrors and visited the chapel, with its beautiful ceiling painted in 1710. On Thursday evening, they visited the Alhambra Theatre in Paris, and as most of the performers were English it was a very enjoyable evening for them. Friday morning was spent visiting the shops, and although they did not have much time to themselves they managed to buy souvenirs for their friends at home. After lunch they placed a beautiful wreath in the Père Lachaise cemetery. They then visited the French Athletic Stadium and had tea before leaving the French capital for Le Havre, where they stayed at the Hôtel Angleterre.

After breakfast on the Saturday morning the team had the more sombre task of laying more wreaths on soldiers' graves before beginning preparations for their afternoon match with the French ladies in Le Havre. A crowd of 10,000, the smallest of the tour, saw Dick, Kerr's record a convincing victory of 6–0, with all the girls playing exceptionally well.

The next day, Sunday 7 November 1920, they left for Rouen at nine o'clock and after checking in at their hotel they were taken on yet another sightseeing tour. They saw the tower where Joan of Arc was imprisoned, and afterwards they returned to the hotel for dinner. On their way to the Lilas Stadium they placed another wreath in memory of allied soldiers who had so bravely given their lives during the conflict.

In the final match of their tour, Dick, Kerr's defeated the French ladies by 2–0 in front of 14,000 spectators. The tour, without doubt, had been an unqualified success, and the ladies achieved their aim of being undefeated in all their matches.

They left Rouen for Dieppe and the return Channel crossing to Newhaven was much smoother than the outward journey. They arrived back at the Bonnington Hotel about eight o'clock for another overnight stay, and the next morning they left Euston on the last leg of their marathon trip. They had covered over 2,000 miles.

On Tuesday 9 November, they arrived back in Preston at six in the evening. As they stepped from the train, they were congratulated by a large crowd of supporters and friends, and as they made their way to the station entrance the Dick, Kerr's band played 'See the Conquering Heroes Come'. Outside, a charabanc was waiting, and as they drove away, the team received a rousing cheer from the crowd. The band marched in front of the charabanc, which made a tour along Fishergate to Lune Street, down Friargate to Marsh Lane, then on to the canteen at the Dick, Kerr works on Strand Road. The team was enthusiastically welcomed by the crowds all along the route, and the players acknowledged their cheers by waving Union Jacks and French tricolours.

At the canteen, they were welcomed by Mr R. Livingstone, the works manager. The players and their friends were the guests of the firm to dinner, over which Mr Livingstone presided. He welcomed the team home and congratulated them on their success. After all the formalities and speechmaking, they were all entertained by members of the Dick, Kerr Pierrot Troupe.

Afterwards, Mr Frankland said that in his personal opinion, the tour had done something towards cementing the Entente Cordiale. According to the *Lancashire Daily Post* he said, 'With the exception of slight colds, the team have returned with a clean bill of health and we have been able to field the same team in every match.'

If they had any complaint, it was that they did not have enough time to see as much of the country as they would have liked. It had been their intention to place floral tributes on the graves of Eddie Latheron of Blackburn Rovers and others, but circumstances had prevented them from doing so. They did, however, discover the grave of one young Preston man, and the girls had covered it with flowers.

So as the tour came to its conclusion, the bond of friendship made between the two teams would see them through the Second World War and continue well into the 1950s, when many more visits would be made between the two countries, with much more money raised for the many worthwhile charities they supported.

Carmen Pomies was another of the French ladies who returned to Preston to play football for Dick, Kerr Ladies. She lived and worked in the town for several years. She was a champion javelin thrower for France and also a versatile footballer who could play either in goal or outfield. The French team returned for a tour of England in May of 1921, and it is likely that Carmen decided to stay in Preston at the end of this team visit. It is also likely that her first game for the Preston team was at Birmingham City FC, on 6 August 1921 against Coventry ladies. The result was a 4–0 victory for Dick, Kerr's.

3 Record Breakers

It was unheard of in the early days of football for the game to be played at night. There were no such things as floodlights for a night-time kick-off; the technology simply was not available. Football by night was a novelty idea, and Dick, Kerr Ladies were once again to be the first to break new ground.

By 20 November 1920 they were back on the road again, this time travelling to Leicester for another fund-raising fixture against St Helen's Ladies, at which 22,000 people saw a 4–0 victory for Dick, Kerr's.

The local charity for Unemployed Ex-Servicemen were in need of food for Christmas, and so it was suggested by Mr Livingstone that Dick, Kerr Ladies play a match by searchlight to help raise much-needed funds for them. They had only ten days to prepare for the game and arrangements were made for it to be played at Deepdale against a team made up of players from the rest of England. Permission was granted from the War Office by the Secretary of State for War, Winston Churchill, for two anti-aircraft searchlights and generating sets to be loaned to them for the occasion, along with forty carbide flares.

The two military searchlights, placed at either end of the ground, threw powerful beams of light above the playing area, and close to the touchline, the forty carbide lights were placed all around the pitch. As there were no white footballs manufactured in those days, Bob Holmes, a former member of the Preston North End 'Old Invincibles' team, kept himself busy whitewashing and throwing a newly painted ball on to the field at regular intervals to enable it to be seen from all parts of the ground.

Bob Holmes, incidentally, was born in Preston in 1867, and he grew up to become the captain both of Preston North End and the Football League XI. He also won seven caps for England. He made his debut for the club in their first ever league game against Burnley in September 1888, and he also played in the FA Cup Final of the same year. An ever-present member of the team, he finally retired from professional football at the end of the 1899/1900 season, but continued to play as an amateur. He was president of the Football Players' Union and later took up refereeing and coaching. Without doubt, Bob Holmes is one of the most celebrated players in the history of Preston North End, yet there he was whitewashing footballs for Dick, Kerr Ladies FC. In his later years he could still been seen around Deepdale, working as an assistant groundsman. He died in his home town in 1955, at the age of eighty-eight.

Owing to an air-lock and a petrol shortage, the searchlights twice went out of action, just before the start, and once during the first half, but even then there was sufficient illumination for the game to be easily followed by both players and spectators.

Along with Pathé News and hoards of pressmen, 10,000 spectators came to witness this unique match on Thursday 17 December 1920. Matches by artificial light had been played by professional men's teams at various times in the past, but according to those present in the crowd who could remember such games, none was as successful as this one turned out to be. The game could hardly have taken place under better conditions. The night was windless and clear, and not cold enough to cause any discomfort. A touch of frost remained on the surface and the pitch was hard, but the game was played at a good pace by both teams.

The Dick, Kerr eleven were the same side which had played in all four games in France: Hastie, Kell, Parr, Woods, Walmsley, Hulme, Haslam, Lyons, Redford, Harris and Clayton.

The game finally kicked off at 7.15 p.m. after the slight delay due to one of the searchlights going out, and in the darkness, little Jennie Harris could not be found, until a cameraman obligingly set off one of his flashlights! Bob Crompton of Blackburn Rovers then started the proceedings, which were refereed by Mr W. Taylor of Longridge.

The Preston side showed an all-round improvement in their performance since they had last appeared in a match in their home town, and the players who were most prominent once more were the famous trio of Harris, Redford and Kell.

There were several amusing incidents during the game. At one point, the operator of the searchlight at the Fulwood end of the ground turned his searchlight on an exciting duel between the Preston forwards and the opposing defence. As a consequence, the players were literally blinded, temporarily losing all sense of position and direction. In addition, the players suffered somewhat in front of goal from the enthusiasm of the press photographers and kinema operators, who, in their endeavour to record the game faithfully, fired off a number of flashlights when a forward was in the act of shooting, leading to some bad finishing.

Jennie Harris, Dick, Kerr's inside-left, finished badly in front of goal from a good scoring position. Her first attempt to find the net was from close range, but to the great amusement of spectators and players alike, her shot travelled so high over the goal that the ball struck the top of the south stand and fell behind it. She soon made up for this error, however, by scoring two goals later in the first half. Florrie Redford and Minnie Lyons also added goals in the last few minutes of the game. Annie Hastie in the Dick, Kerr goal did not have one shot to save all evening. The Rest of England played well enough, but they could not stop the might of Dick, Kerr's as they recorded yet another 4–0 victory. The Rest of Englands' best player on the night was Waine, their goalkeeper from St Helens. She made several excellent saves, even injuring herself in the process.

After the match, both teams and the officials were entertained to supper in the canteen at the Dick, Kerr works, and a vote of thanks was made to all concerned by the representatives from the Unemployed Ex-Servicemen's Distress Fund. They were to receive in excess of £600 as a result of the game.

In 1993, ninety-year-old Charles Newton, who had actually been a spectator at the match, remembered, 'I had never seen lassies play football before, and they were quite adept. They had some very good players and I remember they overplayed the opposition. I thought that Alice Kell was the player most outstanding.'

Undoubtedly the biggest crowd ever to attend a women's football match at club level was the one present on Boxing Day 1920, at Goodison Park, Everton. Mr Frankland had been advised by a gentleman writing in the *Topical Times* that he would raise over £1,000 for charity if he played a game on Merseyside. What occurred that day far exceeded everyone's expectations and will probably stay in the record books for ever.

In the event, there were 53,000 people packed inside Goodison Park, with between 10,000 and 14,000 unable to gain admission. There were so many people about, indeed, that the players had to have a police escort to guide them safely to their changing rooms. They had all come to see Dick, Kerr Ladies play their closest rivals, St Helens Ladies. Both teams had already met seven times that year, with Dick, Kerr's the victors on each occasion. But here were St Helens at home on Merseyside. Could they dent the armour of the invincible Dick, Kerr Ladies in front of their own crowd?

Florrie Redford had missed the train to Liverpool and was therefore unavailable for selection. St Helens must have been hoping they could take advantage of Dick, Kerr's being without one of their best strikers. The game was kicked off by Ella Retford at eleven o'clock.

The diminutive Jennie Harris was moved to centre-forward to try to compensate for the missing firepower of Redford, and at the interval, Dick, Kerr's were leading by 1–0 thanks to a goal scored by her. In the second half, a reshuffle of the team saw Alice Kell, captain and right-back, switched to the centre-forward position. She put on a fine display and scored a remarkable hat-trick, which helped her side to a memorable 4–0 victory.

The Lord Mayor of Liverpool presented the team with a silver cup, while each member of the team received a medal as a gift of thanks from the ex-servicemen's organizations. An amazing total of £3,115 was raised that day for charity, far exceeding the expectations of anyone at the club.

Two weeks later, a match against Bath Ladies was arranged, to be played at Old Trafford, the home of Manchester United. Extra trains, trams and buses were laid on, due to the interest in the game. The Bath side were coached by Charlie Slade, the Huddersfield Town half-back, and they had the reputation of being one of the best teams in the country. It was to be the first meeting between the two clubs.

Another southern team had withdrawn from playing a charity match with Dick, Kerr's because they had refused to weaken their side. Bath Ladies, on the other hand, were anxious to meet the Preston girls at full strength. A crowd of around 35,000 saw yet another victory for Dick, Kerr Ladies with the fourteen-year-old Lily Parr scoring four of her team's goals.

4 1921 – The Highs and Lows

By 1921 the team's popularity was at its height; Dick, Kerr Ladies were the team everyone wanted to see. They had been booked for an average of two games a week all over the British Isles until the middle of August, and there was even talk of a tour to Canada. Many charities had realized what a little goldmine these girls represented and they had been inundated with requests to play. In fact they had received so many requests that regrettably they had to refuse at least 120 invitations from lord mayors and MPs from all parts of the land.

Let no one detract from the dedication these ladies had for their sport. It must have been extremely hard work for them. They were of course giving up all of their Saturdays, and in many cases their holidays too. For midweek matches they had to go to work before travelling to the venue to play the match, and it should not be forgotten that in those days they could not just zoom up or down the motorway to play a fixture.

They used to sing songs to while away the travelling time and they even had a song of their own:

> When upon the field of play we go
> Thousands come to cheer us on our way
> And you will often hear them say
> Who can beat Dick, Kerr's today?
> When the ball is swinging merrily
> Faces are all beaming happily
> So play up girls and do your best
> For victory is our cry.

Alice Norris recalls, 'It was sometimes hard work when we played a match during the week because we would have to work in the morning, travel to play the match, then travel home again and be up early for work the next day. But I was proud to be a Dick, Kerr's girl; it was worth all the effort we put in.'

Harry Weldon, who was a famous comedian in the 1920s, was in Liverpool appearing in the pantomime, *Dick Whittington*, at the Olympia. He had the idea of staging a charity costume (fancy-dress) carnival in aid of unemployed ex-servicemen, Liverpool hospitals and the Variety Artistes' Benevolent Fund.

The carnival was arranged to take place on 14 February 1921, and the directors of Liverpool Football Club gave permission for a ladies' football match to be staged at Anfield in the afternoon. Dick, Kerr Ladies were invited to play against a team made up of the best players from the rest of the country. It was Harry Weldon's idea to get the opposition together in a serious attempt to 'put one over' the invincible Dick, Kerr's team, so the Rest of Britain team was made up of the best individual players in ladies' teams throughout the British Isles; distance was no object. One came from Ireland, two from Wales and one player even came from the Island of Unst in the Shetland Isles. The rest of the team came from all parts of England, such as London, Southampton, Barrow-in-Furness and St Helens.

Both teams were invited to take part in the fancy-dress carnival procession through the streets of Liverpool, starting from the Olympia at twelve noon and proceeding via London Road, Lime Street, Lord Street and other main throughfares to Anfield for the kick-off at three o'clock.

A crowd of 25,000 people came along to see if the invincible Dick, Kerr's could be beaten by the Rest of Britain. The Dick, Kerr team was: Annie Hastie, Alice Kell, Daisy Clayton, Alice Woods, Jessie Walmsley, Lily Lee, Florrie Haslam, Jennie Harris, Florrie Redford, Alice Mills and Lily Parr.

When Ella Retford kicked off the match there seemed to be more photographers than players on the field, newspaper men and moving picture operators (Pathé News) fighting for the best position.

The Preston team soon took control of the game and quickly went into a three-goal lead thanks to a hat-trick from Lily Parr. Riddell, the Scottish centre-forward, scored for the Rest of Britain. Just before half time, Daisy Clayton, the Dick, Kerr left-back, was injured and in need of some treatment. The crowd roared when their lady trainer, Annie Crozier, came on to the field with a sponge and towel to treat the injured player.

Goals came quickly in the second half, with two more for Lily Parr, taking her game total to five. Two came from Florrie Redford and two from Jennie Harris, and the final score was 9–1, yet another emphatic victory for Dick, Kerr Ladies. The fine sum of £1,500 was raised in gate receipts alone. The Preston ladies were justifiably satisfied with their performance against a team representing the best of the rest of Britain.

It was decided not to present the 'Harry Weldon Cup' after the match at Anfield. Instead, the teams and officials were invited to a gala performance of *Dick Whittington* at the Olympia. At the end of the performance the team was invited on to the stage to receive the cup from the man himself. Alice Kell accepted on behalf of the team, and they received a truly wonderful ovation from the audience. (The cup is, to this day, in the possession of Reginald Cook, Alice's son. It is probably the only cup won by the team the whereabouts of which is still known.)

Later the same year, in May, the French team made a welcome return to England, this time playing other teams in the south. They did travel up to Staffordshire, however, where they played Dick, Kerr's in front of 15,000 spectators. Lily Parr scored all five goals in the Preston team's 5–1 victory; the Dick, Kerr's bandwaggon continued to roll.

Everything was not all sweetness and light, however, storm clouds were gathering, and in spite of all its success the team still attracted hostility from the many critics of women's football. Indeed, throughout the life of the sport, the negative opinions of the anti-women's football lobby would rear their ugly heads at regular intervals. It seemed that, according to them, women's football *had* to be stopped at all costs.

There was, first and foremost, resentment building up within the male soccer establishment because of the sheer size of the crowds women's football, and in particular Dick, Kerr's matches could attract. Despite the fact that worthy charities were benefiting from the ladies' matches, the uncomfortable truth was that they were drawing bigger crowds than the men, and the boys simply didn't like it. The green-eyed monster was getting closer to the surface.

Opinions were sought from the medical profession as to the effect football might have on the ladies, and some doctors said that in their 'expert' opinion, football *was* a dangerous pursuit for ladies to follow. They were obviously clutching at straws in their efforts to stop women's football, and it was ludicrous to suggest that it was safe enough for them to run around a hockey pitch yielding a big stick, but that football was definitely not a game for them and that they could do themselves serious harm playing it. There were even suggestions, however, that women would not be able to have children because of playing the sport.

There were also rumours regarding the monies raised at matches and their distribution. Suggestions were made that too much money was being swallowed up by expenses. The smear campaign had started, and the writing was on the wall, but the ladies protested their innocence vehemently. Yes, they received some expenses for loss of time at work or travelling, but they never received a penny more than what they had spent and they were hurt at allegations to the contrary. As far as the ladies were concerned, what happened to the money after the match was nothing to do with them; their interest went no further than what happened on the football pitch. But the finger of suspicion had been pointed at women's football and it was only a matter of time before the bubble burst.

There may have been an element of truth in the allegations concerning the financial side of things, but any irregularities certainly had nothing to do with the ladies. To insult these women publicly by questioning their ability to play a game they had already been playing well for a number of years was therefore quite ridiculous.

In 1921 alone Dick, Kerr Ladies played an amazing total of sixty-seven games of football for charity all over the British Isles, and a staggering number – almost 900,000 people – came to watch them. Small wonder that the men were beginning to panic.

A list of the dates, venues, number of spectators and – where possible – gate receipts of all the games played by Dick, Kerr ladies in 1921 illustrates how much stamina these ladies had. All the games resulted in victories and there were no ill effects to any of the players.

Date	Venue	Crowd	Gate Receipts
1 January	Clitheroe	5,000	?
8	Manchester	33,500	£1,962
22	Great Harwood	5,000	£140
29	Macclesfield	7,000	£385
5 February	Nelson	6,000	£325
8	Stalybridge	12,000	£763
9	Chester	11,000	£700
12	Rossendale	8,000	£500
14	Liverpool	25,000	£1,500
19	Wrexham	10,000	?

26	Coventry	27,000	£2,000
1 March	Glasgow	6,000	?
2	Edinburgh	23,000	£700
5	Burslem	10,000	?
12	Lancaster	8,000	?
19	Hull	20,000	?
25	Dudley	18,000	£700
28	Coventry	12,000	?
29	Cardiff	18,000	?
31	Swansea	25,000	?
6 April	Leeds	27,000	£1,700
7	Stoke	20,000	?
9	Standish	2,000	?
13	Bradford	20,000	£1,150
14	Rotherham	20,000	£1,000
16	Kilmarnock	15,000	£700
19	Bury	27,000	£1,000
20	Bolton	33,000	£1,500
23	New Brighton	15,000	£600
26	Rochdale	18,000	£800
28	Barrow	12,000	£600
4 May	Sheffield	20,000	?
5	Hull	19,000	£900
11	Middlesbrough	25,000	£1,200
14	Preston	12,000	£600
17	Longton, Staffs	15,000	?
21	Nottingham	20,000	£800
4 June	Crewe	10,000	?
1 August	Ramsay IOM	5,000	?
2	Port Erin IOM	6,000	?
3	Douglas IOM	2,000	?
4	Leeds	20,000	?
5	Southport	16,000	?
6	Birmingham	15,000	?
7	Batley	10,000	?
8	Halifax	15,000	?
9	Derby	20,000	?
10 September	Aberdeen	18,000	?
11	Dundee	8,000	£300
12	Bury	3,000	?
13	Birkenhead	6,000	?
14	Rochdale	?	?

15	Blackpool	12,000	?
16	Bristol	8,000	?
17 October	Huddersfield	8,000	?
18	Scarborough	5,000	?
19	Ormskirk	9,000	?
20	Warrington	8,000	?
21	Southport	5,000	?
22	Bradford	10,000	?
23	Dumfries	6,000	?
24	Belfast	12,000	?
25	Wigan	6,000	?
26 November	?	3,000	?
28 December	Preston	3,000	?
29	New Brighton	7,000	?

(All the above information comes from diaries belonging to Mrs Alice Stanley, formerly Alice Woods. The gate receipts for the twenty-five matches listed totals £22,525. The information was actually documented by her husband, Herbert Stanley, who acted in some official capacity for the club during that time. It is not known why all the gate receipts were not listed.)

With such facts in mind, the FA's reasons for their actions seem all the more extraordinary and reveal them in a poor light. The modern-day professional footballer plays an average of forty-two league games per season, plus cup matches, and he does not have to work full-time in a factory as well. Nevertheless, the FA finally dealt a fatal blow to the women's game, effectively changing the face of women's football for ever. On 5 December 1921, the FA unanimously passed the following resoloution:

> Complaints having been made as to football being played by women, the council feel impelled to express their strong opinion that the game of football is quite unsuitable for females and ought not to be encouraged.
>
> Complaints have also been made as to the conditions under which some of these matches have been arranged and played, and the appropriation of receipts to other than charitable objects.
>
> The council are further of the opinion that an excessive proportion of the receipts are absorbed in expenses and an inadequate percentage devoted to charitable objects.

For these reasons the council request clubs belonging to the association to refuse the use of their grounds for such matches.

The axe had fallen, and despite all the ladies' denials and assurances regarding finances, and their willingness to play under any conditions that the FA laid down, the decision was irreversible. The chauvinists, the medical 'experts' and the anti-women's football lobby had won – their precious male bastion was now safe.

Alfred Frankland, secretary and manager, expressed his disgust at the FA's decision, and speaking to the *Lancashire Daily Post* on 6 December 1921, he said that the women's games would continue if organizers of charity matches would provide them with grounds on which to play. With regard to the question of payments to players, he said that Dick, Kerr's only paid travelling expenses, accommodation costs and compensation for loss of time at work. The girls were in no way paid for playing football. Regarding the FA's opinion that the game was not suitable for women, Mr Frankland said that Dick, Kerr Ladies Football Club did not think the FA capable of judging whether the game was dangerous or not.

One of Dick, Kerr's best players was a nurse at Whittingham Hospital. After being on duty all night, in charge of a ward, she would cycle the seven miles to Preston, travel by train to, for example, the Midlands, play a good game of football in the afternoon in front of a record crowd, and be back on duty at the hospital the same evening. She suffered no ill effects from her exertions.

Such examples, however, did not stop the medical profession from voicing their absurd opinions. One doctor was quoted in the *Lancashire Daily Post* of December 1921 as saying, 'I do not believe women are fitted for violent leg strain, and even professional dancing on the stage is objectionable on this account.' A Dr Elizabeth Sloan Chesser was also quoted: 'There are physical reasons why the game is harmful to women. It is a rough game at any time, but it is much more harmful to women than men. They may receive injuries from which they may never recover.' Dr Mary Scharlieb, a Harley Street physician, said, 'I consider it a most unsuitable game, too much for a woman's physical frame.' Mr Eustace Miles said, 'I consider football quite an inappropriate game for most women, especially if they have not been medically tested first.'

Alice Kell, captain and right-back, whose only mishap had been an injury to her wrist caused by a fall while running, was emphatically of the opinion that girls should have the right to play football if they so wished. She was also quoted in the *Lancashire Daily Post*:

> We play for the love of the game and we are determined to carry on. It is impossible for working girls to afford to leave work to play matches all over the country and be the losers. I see no reason why we shouldn't be recompensed for loss of time at work. No one ever receives more than ten shillings per day.

The ladies were convinced that the FA had taken this action because they were drawing much bigger crowds than the men, and there can be no doubt that this was one of the reasons. The case for the women was put very fairly in a letter which a Major Cecil Kent, of Liverpool, sent to the secretary of the FA, at whose meeting it was read. In his letter, printed in the *Lancashire Daily Post* of 6 December 1921 Major Kent, a former secretary of the Old Westminsters FC, said:

> I may mention that in present and past seasons I have watched about 30 ladies football matches between various teams and I have met the players. I have travelled with them frequently by road and rail and I have attended the various functions to which they have been invited, and I have met the the lord mayors and also the officials of the local charities and football clubs concerned. On all sides I have heard nothing but praise for the good work the girls are doing and the high standard of their play. The only thing I now hear from the man in the street is, 'Why have the FA got their knife into girls' football? What have the girls done except to raise large sums for charity and to play the game? Are their feet heavier on the turf than the men's feet?'

But the financial side of things was an altogether murkier area. Was there some unscrupulous person or persons taking advantage of women's football for their own gain? Apparently, what would happen was this. The secretary/manager of a team would estimate their costs for travel, accommodation and loss of time at work, and then claim this amount from the gate receipts from the charity for which they were playing. The secretary/manager would then reimburse the girls their expenses.

Lydia Ackers, a St Helen's player later transferred to Dick, Kerr's, remembered vividly some interesting facts. Lydia says, 'Well, there won't be many people remember this, but I witnessed it and this is the truth. We were playing a match near Manchester against the West Cheshire's. As we were getting dressed, the man who had brought the West Cheshire team came in and asked how much we got when we played. We told him ten shillings each match. But he was asking for much more. The team he brought to play against us were supposed to be the West Cheshire's but we didn't recognize them. He must have thought that because there had been a big crowd at the game, he would put in for a big lump sum and get more than he was entitled to, but he didn't get it. It wasn't long after this that the FA stopped us from using league grounds.'

At the time of the FA ban, Mr Frankland claimed that Dick, Kerr Ladies had already raised something like £50,000 for charity in the four years they had been playing. Once again, by today's standards, this is a staggering amount of money. There is no question that a tremendous amount of suffering was eased due to the efforts of everyone connected with this wonderful club. It is an achievement of which they can all be proud, and they deserve all the recognition it is possible to give for this feat.

Alfred Frankland went on record stating that it was a resolution of their club committee never to apply for a ground for a charity match. Those responsible for the charity must make all the arrangements themselves and accept all responsibility for payments made regarding the match. Extracts from the minutes of meetings of the Preston North End board of 1918 (referred to in Chapter 1), however, contradict Mr Frankland on this point. Referring to a game played at Deepdale on 23 February 1918, the North End board said: 'We take charge of the gate and pay over to Dick, Kerr & Co. 80 per cent of the net gate.' It is also minuted that the ground was let on the same terms as this for games played on 9 March and the Good Friday of 1918. Whether this policy was adopted for the remainder of their home games at Deepdale is not known, but it is clearly documented that Dick, Kerr Ladies *did* rent Deepdale for the 1918–19 season. It was their committee who approached North End for the use of the ground, and *not* the charity for which they were playing.

There also remains the discrepancy referred to in Chapter 1 regarding the first four games ever played by the club and how much was raised at each game. Mr Frankland stated that the fine sum of £804 10s 5d was raised from those four games £800 coming from the two games with Coulthard's and Bolton, but there is no record of gate receipts for the other two games with a combined gate of 7,000 people. Is it possible that only £4 10s 5d, the remaining sum, was raised from these two games?

It has already been stated that at the time of the FA ban on women's football, Dick, Kerr's had raised something like £50,000 for charity in their four-year history. In 1921 they played sixty-seven matches, and for twenty-five of these, the gate receipts were documented in the diaries belonging to Alice Stanley. The total for gate receipts at these matches was £22,525. For the remaining forty-five matches that year there is no record of any of the gate receipts. Is it fair to assume that the other forty-five games would have brought in at least the same as the twenty-five which were documented? If so, the sum of £50,000 could have been raised in one year alone!

The question then has to be asked: if £50,000 was raised in 1921 alone, how much was raised in the previous three years, what, if anything happened to it, and exactly how much money is unaccounted for?

There are no answers to any of these questions, but it is obvious that the figures simply do not add up.

The ladies, however, wasted no time after the ban, continuing to play the game they loved. On 26 December 1921, three weeks after the FA's momentous decision, Dick, Kerr Ladies welcomed Fleetwood Ladies to their first home game at 'Lively Polly' corner on Ashton Park, Preston. They invited local members of the medical profession to witness the game, which was played in aid of local poor children. It was noted that all the arrangements for the match had been made without any expense whatsoever falling on the gate receipts, and that consequently every penny taken would go to the poor children.

Because of the controversy caused by the statement from the FA as to the unsuitability of football for women, about twenty members of the medical profession accepted the invitation to come along and see at first hand what effect the game had on the ladies.

Fleetwood Ladies were considered among the best teams in women's football, and a crowd of 3,000 came along to witness another victory for the home team by 3–1. Dick, Kerr's were always the superior side and their goals were scored by Lily Parr, Florrie Redford and Jennie Harris. The Dick, Kerr team was: Grice,

Walmsley, Clayton, Pomies, Woods, Lee, Haslam, Harris, Redford, Mills and Parr.

The *Lancashire Daily Post* reporter who covered the match asked the doctors for their opinions as to the safety of the game as played by women. None of them had any adverse criticism and the general opinion was that football was physically no more harmful for women than either tennis or hockey.

After the match, Dr Mary Lowry, who had earlier kicked off the game said, 'From what I saw, football is no more likely to cause injuries to women than a heavy day's washing.' A nonconformist minister who was also present added, 'There is nothing to disapprove of in women's football.' In fact, all the doctors were unanimous: it was in no way harmful for women to play football.

In spite of the FA ban, the public still turned up in their thousands to watch women's football. At New Brighton on 27 December, 7,000 people went along to watch St Helens play Dick, Kerr's. The Preston team recorded another 2–0 victory, with goals scored by Alice Woods and Jennie Harris. Alice Kell had sent out invitations to members of the FA council to attend the match but, not surprisingly, there is no mention of their having attended.

As the new year approached there was much work to be done if women's football was to continue on its own. No one knew what lay ahead; the future was profoundly uncertain. But Dick, Kerr Ladies were determined to forge ahead as they always had done in the past, and new challenges for them were just around the corner.

5 Across the Atlantic

Dick, Kerr Ladies started the new year with the same enthusiasm they had always displayed as the new era of women's football got under way. They may no longer have been allowed the use of association football pitches, but as one door closed another one opened, and among other venues, they began playing on rugby grounds.

On 7 January 1922 Dick, Kerr Ladies played on Wakefield Trinity Rugby Football Ground. In front of 8,000 people they played Heys Brewery Ladies from Bradford in aid of the Wakefield Workpeople's Hospital and raised £250 for them. The match ended in a 1–1 draw, with Florrie Redford scoring the Dick, Kerr goal and ending a remarkable run of results. Out of their last 100 games, Dick, Kerr's had won ninety-nine, their last draw being against the French in Paris in October 1920. Heys Brewery Ladies were the champions of Yorkshire and were emerging as a fine side, as their draw with Dick, Kerr's illustrates.

The opposition of the FA to women's football had only increased the women's determination to continue playing the game, and towards the end of 1921, the *Lancashire Daily Post* reported that a Ladies' Football Association had been formally inaugurated at a meeting in Liverpool towards the end of 1921. It also stated that a league of women's clubs was to be formed in the Doncaster area and another in the Coventry area. An East Riding and North Lincolnshire league was also being considered. Dick, Kerr Ladies had heard nothing regarding the Liverpool meeting, and Mr Frankland planned to go there in an endeavour to glean some information about it, though whether he actually did so or not is not known.

If women's football were to succeed on its own without the support of the FA it needed to get its house in order. Representatives of some sixty clubs were therefore scheduled to meet in Manchester to draft rules and decide upon modifications of the game, which were to include the possibility of a slightly smaller playing area and a lighter ball.

This transitional period within the sport was not as easily negotiated as had been hoped, and what became of the Ladies' Football Association in not known. The women were angry at the treatment that had been meted out to them, and without the resources and readily available football pitches and officials, it would have been virtually impossible to sustain a national league. What is clear, however, is that for the next fifty years it remained extremely difficult for women to play football because of the FA ban.

It was easier for teams like Dick, Kerr's who had the support and backing of a big company and did not have to struggle to find a pitch to play on every week. Other teams, who were less fortunate, eventually fell by the wayside. But there were still many charitable organizations in need of help and Dick, Kerr Ladies were more than happy to give their services.

In March 1922 they entertained the French Ladies on yet another of their visits to Preston. One of the matches with the French visitors was played at Burnley, and despite the ban by the FA there was still a lot of support and admiration for women's football. In an extract from a letter to Mr Livingstone, the Dick, Kerr works manager, the Mayor of Burnley, Mr Edwin Whitehead, clearly expresses his support for the team: 'I love your team of Preston lasses, and whenever I find them within a measurable distance of Burnley you may rest assured I shall be at the match if at all possible. They are so cheerful that it does one good to be about them.'

Meanwhile the seeds planted early in 1921 for a proposed trip to Canada were to come to fruition in September of 1922. By this time, women's football was in sore need of a lift, and the ladies of Dick, Kerr's, ever the pioneers, were once more to give the game the boost it needed.

They sailed from Liverpool aboard the SS *Montclare*, a ship of the Canadian Pacific line, on her maiden voyage across the Atlantic to Canada and the United States of America. They were expecting to be away for four months, returning in 1923 after playing a total of twenty-four matches, both in Canada and the United States. In a newspaper clipping in Alfred Frankland's scrapbook, Alice Kell was quoted as saying, just before their departure, that the FA did not approve of their trip and they had even tried to stop them from going but had failed: 'They certainly

Pawtucket, USA, 1922.
Left to right: Florrie Haslam, Molly Walker, Alice Woods,
Jennie Harris, Alice Kell, Lily Lee, Flo Redford, Jessie Walmsley,
Lily Parr, Carmen Pomies, Daisy Clayton.

even tried to stop them from going but had failed: 'They certainly rule English football, but not the world, thank goodness.'

The team on this momentous journey was: Florrie Haslam, Molly Walker, Alice Woods, Jennie Harris, Alice Kell, Lily Lee, Florrie Redford, Jessie Walmsley, Lily Parr, Carmen Pomies, Daisy Clayton, Alice Mills, Annie Crozier, May Graham, Lily Stanley and R. J. Garrier. Their regular goalkeeper, Peggy Mason, was unable to go with the team due to the sad loss of her mother.

Alice Woods recalls the extremely rough Atlantic crossing and remembers that most of the girls were seasick. She also recalls that they saw some beautiful icebergs and that these reminded them of the *Titanic*. Despite the fear of emulating that doomed ship, however, nothing could prevent the women from undertaking the biggest adventure of their lives. And during the voyage the Dick, Kerr girls were introduced to the French heavyweight boxer, Georges Carpentier, who was travelling to America to fight Jack Dempsey.

Also among the party on this historic trip was twenty-one-year old Herbert Stanley, who helped out at the club in the capacity as coach and secretary. He actually acted as the team's linesman throughout the tour of the United States. Sadly, Herbert passed away in the 1960s, but he left a tape-recording relating an incident which occurred on board the SS *Montclare*:

> All the arrangements for the tour had been in the hands of an American Jew and an Irish international football player who happened to be captain of a famous north of England club. He will be nameless. He was a very fit, fine, upstanding figure of a man; good-looking, curly hair and I was eventually apportioned the same cabin as him when we got on board ship. There were only two classes, cabin and what was known as second class. We travelled cabin.
>
> David – I'll refer to him as David – was, I afterwards learned, a man who had left his wife and family and cleared the country without saying a word. He had been doing all the negotiating for the tour in secret, and this was his getaway.
>
> I first met him when we were on board the ship. He was a likeable fellow. I didn't know his history or his background except through the press and his football career. His one ambition in life, I soon learned, was to make love to women, any woman, provided he could gain his own ends.

And there was I thrown with him for a period of ten days on this ship!

Two days out we hit a heavy storm and most of the passengers were seasick, but on the third day all began to recover and the life of the ship went on.

David, I learned, was broke. Now in those days, before you could land in Canada you had to have in your possession at least £25 in English money. I knew David had nothing, but he said, 'Don't worry.' He was happy and carefree, he didn't mind. He would make out.

He asked me how much money I had and I told him that I didn't have £25 either. I personally didn't know how I was going to get through the immigration authorities when we got to the other side. He asked again, 'Well, how much have you got?' I told him, and by his charming manner, he borrowed £2 from me.

I didn't see much of him for the next two or three days except at mealtimes, but I knew he was making love to an elderly woman, a very rich woman, and the way he was carrying on anyone would have thought they were teenagers!

Dick, Kerr Ladies were well known and their autographs were sought, and it was one of my duties to see that autographed photographs of the team were sold for charity or given to important people whenever possible.

One day, soon after breakfast, David came to me and said, 'When I beckon you on deck, come to me and stand between the cabin behind, and where I am stood. I'll tell you my reasons for it afterwards.' Sure enough, he had his lady love engaged in the usual loving dialogue, leaning over the ship's rail. Presently, he pulled out his wallet, extracted one of the photographs of the team and said he would get all the players to autograph the picture for her and would start off with his name. He called me over and I stood where he had told me to stand, and he said, 'Will you get this photograph signed by the rest of the party?' I said I would. He half turned, and with a deft flick of his right wrist, he flicked his wallet into the sea, with a cry, 'My wallet!' I was the only one who had seen this action. He had attracted the attention of some of the crew and a number of the passengers and we all watched the wallet as it was swallowed up in the waves. Then came the most pathetic story you have ever heard about him being destitute; his world of wealth was in that wallet, how would he pass the authorities at the other side?

The purser organized a collection amongst the first-class passengers, and when David was asked how much he had in the wallet he said it was just over £50. The collection raised about £45, and during the dance on deck that night the money that had been collected was presented to David. With grateful thanks and with something of an apologetic manner, he said the remainder of the money did not matter.

In the cabin later that night he returned me my £2. The whole of his scheme had been really well organized, and looking back I feel that for a most plausible rogue, David took the cake.

The team arrived in Quebec on Friday 22 September 1922, and were met by a Mr Zelickman of the Brooklyn Football Club from New York. Mr Zelickman was the joint promoter of the tour along with a Mr David Brooks. It is probably a safe assumption that Mr Zelickman, and David Brooks, were the American Jew and the Irish international football player mentioned at the beginning of Herbert Stanley's story. What happened to David Brooks after the tour is unknown.

The organization for the tour was a mess. By 2 September 1922, only one match had been arranged in Canada against Grand Trunk from Montreal, scheduled for 28 October. The *Toronto Evening Telegram* had reported that Dick, Kerr Ladies were anxious to play in Toronto before their return to England. The paper seemed to be under the impression that the ladies were already in the United States when in fact they were still in England. The information must have come from the organizers of the tour in the States, and it was said that they (the tour organizers) were asking for a guarantee fee of $1,000 for the team to play there.

If this sort of money was raised during the tour, it is surely legitimate to ask whose pockets it went into. There is certainly no mention in any of the newspaper reports of any funds being donated to charity. Other familiar problems followed the team across the Atlantic.

Extracts from the minutes of the AGM of the Dominion Football Association (DFA), held in Winnipeg on 5 September 1922, read as follows:

> Arising out of a letter from the United States regarding the proposed tour of footballers into this country, President MacNeil wanted to know whether ladies' football was to be approved of or not.
>
> Mr Steven did not approve of ladies' football.
>
> Mr Lyne was also against ladies' football.
>
> Mr Swain desired to know the reason of disapproval.
>
> In reply, Mr Lyne said that a woman was not built to stand the bruises gotten in playing football.
>
> Mr Dean quoted an instance of ladies' football having been played in Hamilton. He said that the first two games played were all right, but after that the people became against it entirely. He regarded it as a shame to be allowed. He thought such games should not be permitted.
>
> Moved by Mr Lyne, seconded by Mr Dean, that we do not approve of the proposal of ladies' football. Carried.
>
> Mr Steven, seconded by Mr Russell, wished to go on record as not approving of ladies' football. This was consented to.
>
> Moved by Mr Mitchell, seconded by Mr Lyne, that we join with the Football Association and pay fee for same.

This 'fee' is not explained, but the mention of the 'Football Association' could refer to the FA in England. If this is the case it does look as if the DFA were encouraged by London to stop the tour.

Upon the team's arrival in Quebec, Mr Zelickman informed the Dick, Kerr party that he had received the cold shoulder from the DFA and they had refused to grant their permission for the team to play football in Canada. He said that he had not been officially notified of this fact by the DFA, but the affiliated clubs in the association had informed him that they were forbidden to play against the visiting English women.

Mr Frankland and the team felt they were owed some kind of explanation from the DFA, and they were most upset and offended at the attitude taken by them. They were all looking forward to visiting Niagara Falls and other Canadian tourist attractions, but unfortunately they were robbed of the opportunity. Unbeknownst to the visitors, there had been even more skulduggery afoot. The FA could not stop them making the trip but they could and did certainly try to prevent them from playing football. It does seem likely that the FA in England had been instrumental in forcing the cancellation of plans to extend the tour throughout Canada. The DFA had already frowned upon the proposed visit of the women soccer players and were clearly happy to oblige London by preventing the ladies playing. If we read between the lines, it becomes sickeningly apparent that the men at the FA would stop at nothing in order to prevent women playing football.

Mr Zelickman also informed the visitors that during the tour they would be expected to play against men's teams and not against ladies, as had been understood when they left England. He must, however, surely have been aware of this before the party set sail, as must David Brooks. The reasons given for this stipulation were that there was a shortage of women's teams with enough experience and ability to play against Dick, Kerr's. (In truth, there probably were no women's teams at all, otherwise fixtures would surely have been arranged for them.) So it was suggested that instead of playing against other ladies, they should play against men's teams in exhibition matches. Under great pressure, they agreed to do this, but they had little alternative. It was a *fait accompli* and so they all resigned themselves to the inevitable, regarding the tour as an experiment.

They were accompanied to New York by Mr Zelickman of Brooklyn FC, and they began their tour of the Atlantic coast states. Unfortunately the team's bookings had not been handled properly and plans for games in Chicago, Detroit, Cleveland and other midwestern states had to be cancelled.

The finances, scheduling and other details of the tour, organized by the management of Brooklyn FC, became so muddled that in order to protect the visitors from being stranded in the country, Thomas Bagnall (representing the USFA) assumed control of the team. Up to that point they had been unhappy with the arrangements, and some of their hotels were infested with cockroaches. It was at their request that Mr Bagnall took charge of the tour, and from then on things improved greatly.

Their first game in the United States was played on Sunday 24 September 1922, against Paterson FC, at the Olympic Park, Clifton, New Jersey, in front of 5,000 spectators. The team line-up was: Carmen Pomies, Alice Kell, Lily Lee, Molly Walker, Alice Woods, Jessie Walmsley, Florrie Haslam, Jennie Harris, Flo Redford, May Graham, Lily Parr.

As a result of a misunderstanding, the team had been wrongly heralded as Newcastle United Ladies FC, but this may have been due to the famous black-and-white shirts worn by the Dick, Kerr team. In any event, the crowd gave a tremendous welcome to the ladies from Preston as they entered the arena to the sound of loud cheering and the tooting of horns. The girls put up a gallant fight in their first match in America, but lost the game 6–3. The Dick, Kerr goals were scored by Redford, Walmsley and Parr. Jennie Harris was among those given good reports in the *New York Times*, as were Lily Parr, Alice Kell, Flo Redford and Carmen Pomies.

Soccer was a new sport in the United States and the average attendance at a men's game was about 4,000. The ladies, however, played before crowds of between 4,000 and 10,000, and they were told that these attendances exceeded those achieved when Third Lanark FC, from Scotland, had recently toured there.

As it had been autumn when they had left home, the women had all taken clothing more suited to the English climate. Upon their arrival in America, however, they found that it was much too warm for the clothes they were wearing, so one of their first shopping trips was to rush out and buy something cooler to wear! They were also fascinated by all the electrical appliances in use in America. It was, for example, the first time they had ever seen an electric washing machine, as these were not yet widely available in England.

Their second match was played on Saturday 30 September, at Pawtucket, Rhode Island, against J. & P. Coats FC, in front of 8,500 spectators. The crowd gave a rousing cheer as the Dick, Kerr team marched on to the field to the strains of 'Annie Laurie'. It was a warm day and the heat of the sun affected the girls performance, but Lily Parr was outstanding and she kept the fans entertained with her skill and strength of shot. Despite the heat, the girls did manage a 4–4 draw, with goals coming from Redford (two), Harris and Parr.

The next day, the girls were once again taking to the field, this time at the New York Oval, New York City. They took on Centro-Hispano FC, a team made up of Spanish Americans, in front of a crowd of 7,000. At the start of the game a large bouquet of flowers was presented to Flo Redford, who was acting captain in place of Alice Kell. A brass band played the American and British national anthems.

Defeated they eventually were, but by no means humiliated for with only twenty-four hours between their game in Pawtucket and the one in New York, they showed remarkable speed and staying power against the Centro-Hispano eleven, who were runners-up in the Metropolitan Football League. After going down 2–0 early in the game, at the half-time whistle the Dick, Kerr team were leading by 3–2, their clever passing having regularly brought them salvos of applause from the crowd. During the match Lily Lee, playing at left-back, was injured in a collision with one of the Hispano players and was knocked out. When they realized she was unable to get up, her team-mates rushed to help her and she was soon back on her feet again, thanks to the help of Annie Crozier, the team trainer. The Centro-Hispanos lost no time in equalizing and soon made it 4–3. The final score was 7–5 to the Hispanos. The scorers for the ladies were Flo Redford (two) May Graham, Jennie Harris and Lily Parr.

Sunday 8 October saw them take on Washington Stars FC in Washington DC. The result was a 4–4 draw. On Tuesday 10 October they arrived in New Bedford, having made the trip from Washington. They were entertained to a banquet organized by the officials of the soccer leagues in the city. The *Fall River Evening Herald* reported that the team were being coached by David Brooks.

In New Bedford, Massachusetts, on Thursday 12 October, Dick, Kerr Ladies defeated the New Bedford Allstars at Sargent's Field by 5–4 in front of 6,000 people. The New Bedford team had a collection of all stars picked from some of the best players in the city. A storm of applause greeted the girls as they were led on to the field by Alice Kell. It was the biggest crowd ever seen at Sargent's Field. The Allstars entered the game not giving enough respect to the skill of the Preston team, and it was clear they were not taking the game too seriously. When it came time to go out and get the goals, however, the New Bedford team found that the ladies could defend as well as go forward, and try as they might they could not break down the solid Dick, Kerr defence. The ladies' goals came from Redford (two) Harris (two) and Molly Walker. The team also went on to a remarkable victory against New York FC in New York City on Saturday 14 October, where they recorded a scoreline of 8–4.

The *Fall River Evening Herald* reported:

> The Dick, Kerr team is one of the biggest things in soccer ever to have visited the United States. Fall River has seen many championship games yet there has never been a

ladies' club play in this city. It was decided that the public of Fall River should be given the opportunity to see them and so the Dick, Kerr team was booked to play here at an enormous expense. The team has had many other offers and were asked to come to this city before fulfilling their other engagements. Advice from other cities where the team have played warrants that the fans will be given a wonderful show for their money. And other reports say that the team is near perfection in every aspect of the kicking game.

Carmen Pomies was compared with one of the best goalkeepers in the area, Jennie Harris won praise in every game she played, and Lily Parr was said to be capable of showing any of the big leaguers a thing or two! Fall River were taking no chances with this combination and the team's best players were to take the field against the ladies.

At St Mark's Stadium, Tiverton, Fall River, Massachusetts, on Sunday 15 October, Dick, Kerr Ladies duly earned a 2–2 draw with Fall River FC in front of 4,000 spectators. Both goals were scored by Flo Redford. The match report in the local paper said that the men were willing to let the girls win the game, saying that:

> Of course the girls were no match for the men. For girls they are very good and each one clearly showed that she had had considerable experience. However, their visit has helped to promote soccer immensely but the fans would have liked to have seen them play against a women's team. In that case, their skill would have been more evident.

On Sunday 22 October, they recorded another victory by 4–3, when in Baltimore, Maryland, they took on Baltimore SC.

It was reported that the visitors had departed from New York on 26 October, and returned to England aboard the SS *Scythia*. There must have been a change of plan, however, as their last match of the tour was played in Philadelphia on 4 November 1922, at the Baseball Ground. The result was a 5–4 defeat for the ladies. There was a seating capacity of 45,000 and the ground was the best in America. The ladies had never seen so many motor cars at a match before. The American standard of living, they saw, was much better than in England, as nearly all the workers seemed to have their own cars and telephones.

Before the game at the Baseball Ground, four members of the Dick, Kerr team raced the American women's Olympic team in a relay race of about a quarter of a mile. The Preston team comprised Florrie Haslam, Jennie Harris, Molly Walker and Lily Parr. The Preston girls led all the way. Molly Walker established a lead of about three yards, which was slightly reduced against Lily Parr. Jennie Harris increased it again to three yards, but the last American runner made a great effort a few yards from the tape, which Florrie Haslam breasted just before her. The lassies from Lancashire were well pleased with their victory over the Olympic team; it was an achievement for them to be proud of, and it spoke volumes for their level of fitness.

The whole trip was to last for nine weeks and during that time, they played nine matches, won three, drew three and lost three. They all thought the tour had been a great success, but felt that the game was best played against other women's teams. There were no injuries to any of the players, however, and in fact while they were in America, they heard of more injuries to women playing basketball and hockey than they had heard about regarding women playing football. Girls at some colleges in America were learning to play soccer, and there was therefore a possibility that teams would be formed. They visited two such colleges in Baltimore.

While they were being shown around one of the colleges, some male students were out practising their skills in American football. One of the players inadvertently kicked the ball towards Mr Frankland, who was walking through the grounds with some of the Dick, Kerr girls and the boys' team coach. Lily Parr instinctively kicked the oval-shaped ball back towards them, and although she had never kicked a ball of that shape before, she sent it way over the posts. The coach thought this was the biggest fluke of all time and was of the opinion that Lily could not repeat the action. 'How many dollars will you bet?' asked Mr Frankland. The coach shouted to one of the players to kick the ball back towards Lily. Once again, she returned the ball, but this time kicked it even further, leaving the coach-open mouthed in amazement!

During their stay, they also watched two or three men's matches, and were firmly of the opinion that the standard of soccer was not as good as in England. Alice Kell said in the *Lancashire Daily Post*:

> In America football isn't the same game as ours. There isn't the same combination. It's all individual play out there. They don't pass the ball around like we do, so the players all try to go through on their own. The American

players have a style of their own. When a forward is coming along with the ball the full-back doesn't bother much about the ball if he can get the man. In all the games we saw, we noticed this feature.

They were all of the opinion that if only Preston North End had been there, they would really have shown the Americans how to play!

As a rule women did not attend soccer matches in the States, but there were always a lot of ladies at the Dick, Kerr games. And the hospitality everywhere was magnificent, especially in New Bedford and Pawtucket, Rhode Island, where there were a lot of people from Preston who had emigrated to the USA. Throughout the tour, Lily Parr was always an outstanding player. The newspapers reported her as the most brilliant female player in the world, though Flo Redford was the leading goal scorer.

As for the teams the ladies played against, it has to be said that they were some of the best teams in the United States at that time, with many of the players having had experience in the Football League. On the Fall River team, Harold Brittan, the centre-forward, had played for Chelsea at one time and Alec Lorimer, the inside-left, had played for Kilmarnock. The J. & P. Coats team of Pawtucket, Rhode Island, won the championship of the Professional American Soccer League in the 1922–23 season. The inside-right, Fred Morley, had played for Blackpool and Brentford before emigrating, while outside-left Tommy Fleming had played for Morton. The outside-right for the J. & P. Coats team, James Gallagher, later played for the US in the World Cup of 1930 in Montevideo, Uruguay.

The late Pete Renzulli, who played in goal for the Paterson club, a member of the National Hall of Fame, a US international and American Pro League player during the 1920s, commenting on the play of Dick, Kerr Ladies, said: 'Here is something. I played against them in 1922 in goal for the Paterson club. We were national champions and we had a hell of a job beating them 6–3.'

The newspapers reported that the Dick, Kerr Ladies showed remarkable spirit in their games even though they were pitted against some of the strongest men's clubs in the country. They displayed great stamina, clever combination play and considerable speed. The individual performances of several players compared favourably with the skills of the men, Lily Parr in particular displaying great speed and terrific kicking power.

They left New York aboard the SS *Adriatic* on 9 November 1922, and arrived home in England at Liverpool on Friday 17 November. On Friday 1 December they were officially welcomed home from the tour by the management of Dick, Kerr & Co. Ltd (now known as English Electric Ltd due to a recent change at the company) at a social evening and dance, held in the works canteen, appropriately decorated for the occasion. The guest list read like a who's who of local dignitaries.

The *Lancashire Daily Post* reported that Mr Livingstone, the works manager, speaking on behalf of the whole management team, said that they were glad to see their players again and noticed that all the girls looked well after their strenuous American tour. He added that the company were very proud of the charitable services of the club and that they hoped in future that the team would again give their services generously in aid of deserving causes.

Councillor Ellison said he was also delighted to be able to welcome the players home. Some people, he pointed out, did not like ladies playing football, but a subject on which the medical profession disagreed must be judged by laymen, and he felt it was right and proper for ladies to play football, especially in support of charitable institutions.

Alderman Whitehead, ex-Mayor of Burnley, said he was sorry the FA had placed a ban on women's football, and he hoped they would soon see the error of their ways. This was of course met with cries of 'hear, hear' from all present.

The team had brought back with them not only a football signed by President Harding but also an American flag. Mr Frankland hailed the tour as a great success, but admitted it had been badly managed by those on the other side, citing the fact that the players had to make long journeys immediately prior to games. They were, however, greeted with remarkable enthusiasm everywhere they went. He also said it had been a great shock for them when they arrived in Quebec to learn that they had to play against men's teams. The players had made the decision to play the men on their own and they had given a magnificent account of themselves.

The DFA must have had a change of heart regarding their refusal to let Dick, Kerr Ladies play football in Canada, for Mr Livingstone announced, at the welcome-home party, that they had received an offer from Edmonton requesting that the part of the tour which had had to be curtailed should be continued in Canada and the States the following autumn.

One of the players who gave up the game soon after their return from the American tour was Alice Woods, and in 1927, she married Herbert Stanley, whom she had met while playing football for Dick, Kerr's. Some sixty years later, Alice was to find new fame as Mrs Alice Stanley, when she became a celebrity all over again as the thirst for the history of women's football came to the fore. In the 1980s, TV documentaries were eager to chart the beginnings of the women's game, and in particular the world-famous Dick, Kerr Ladies. Alice was taken back to Goodison Park, Everton, where she had played in that record-breaking match against St Helens Ladies. There must have been some wonderful memories for her as she relived those far-off days when Dick, Kerr Ladies were the best in the land. It was thanks to Channels 4's coverage of women's football that Alice was also the guest of honour at several Women's FA Cup finals in the new era of the women's game, and she loved every minute of it.

Alice had won a gold medal while playing for Dick, Kerr Ladies in the 1920s, a medal she treasured and wore around her neck every day for the rest of her life. She died peacefully at her home in Manchester in 1991; she was ninety-two years old.

6 A New Era

Following their successful tour of America, and some of the ladies giving up playing football, there began a time of rebuilding at the club. New players joining the team in 1923 included Hilda Parkinson and Lily Buxton. Both girls came from Blackpool and the two could often be seen practising their footballing skills together on the beach. Lily Buxton was reputed to have given up a career on the stage as a dancer to play football for Dick, Kerr Ladies. She was a member of the John Tiller troupe of dancers (the Tiller Girls) and she had appeared at the Winter Gardens in her home town.

Lizzy Ashcroft and Lydia Ackers came over from St Helens. There was no work for them in their home town, and in Preston they not only found work at Dick, Kerr and Co. Ltd, but they could also play football, the game they both loved. Lizzy, who was nickmaned 'Tommy' by her team-mates, played full-back and was rated the best since Alice Kell. Years later Lizzy's son, Alec Bolton, remembered: 'My mother was a very good player. She used to embarrass me by her skills. I would be playing football in the street with a bunch of kids, and many a time she would come home laden down with shopping bags in each hand, but she could easily take the ball off us, dribble round the kids and score a goal.'

The French Ladies came over again in 1923 for what had now become more or less an annual event, and during this tour they played against the Dick, Kerr Ladies at Cardiff Arms Park. Part of the proceeds of this game were for the Rheims Cathedral Fund in France.

Also in 1923, they played a match as part of the Blackpool Carnival at Squires Gate, against a representative team made up of the rest of the United Kingdom. Prior to the game they took part in the carnival procession on a float. During the parade the team were touched and honoured by a gesture made by the ex-servicemen representing their association on another float in

Cardiff Arms Park, 1923.
Back (left to right): Daisy Clayton, Carmen Pomies,
Alice Woods, Miss Grice?, Alice Kell, Jessie Walmsley.
Front (left to right): Florrie Haslam, Jennie Harris,
Flo Redford, Alice Norris, Lily Parr.

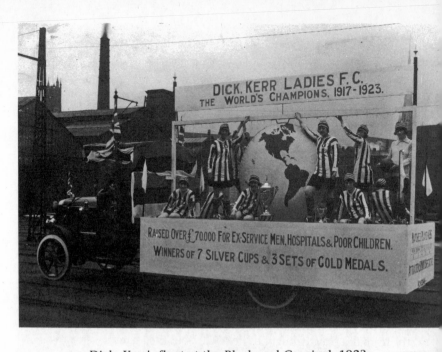

Dick, Kerr's float at the Blackpool Carnival, 1923.

Souvenir programme for the game played at the carnival.

SOUVENIR PROGRAMME.

AS

ᘓᘏ LADIES' FOOTBALL MATCH. ᘓᘏ

Dick Kerr International Ladies v. Rest of United Kingdom. SQUIRES GATE, BLACKPOOL, JUNE 13th, 1923.

Kick off by **HIS WORSHIP THE MAYOR** at 7 p.m.

Referee: Mr. W. SMITH. (London).   Linesmen: Mr. J. WILLIAMS (West Hartlepool); Mr. F. CARROL (Manchester).

DICK KERR'S TEAM.	REST OF UNITED KINGDOM
English Colours: White Jerseys, Black Shirts.	

DICK KERR'S TEAM.

English Colours: White Jerseys, Black Shirts.

Miss A. KELL (Captain).

Miss D. CLAYTON.   Miss L. LEE.

Miss A. NORRIS.   Miss ASHCROFT.   Miss MARTIN.

Miss F. HASLAM.   Miss FRANKLAND.   Miss CHORLEY.
Miss PARR.   Miss ACKERS.

REST OF UNITED KINGDOM

Miss LAMPREY
(Wales).

Miss BRIXTON   Miss McNEIL
(England).   (Scotland).

Miss COLLINSON   Miss McKENNA   Miss BROWN
(England).   (Ireland).   (England).

Miss SHAW   Miss CUTLER   Miss McMONIN   Miss JON
(England).   (England).   (Scotland).   (Wales).
Miss PARKINSON (England).

Our Special Thanks are due to the Ministry of Pensions and Colonel Shea and Staff for valuable assistance rendered.

the carnival. Alice Norris explains: 'Our waggon was going down the road one way and the ex-servicemen were coming up the other way. They stopped adjacent to our float and when they saw us, they stood up and saluted. We all thought how nice it was for them to acknowledge us in this way and we felt very proud. We had raised a lot of money for the Ex-Servicemen's Association through playing football, and we thought perhaps it was their way of saying thank-you.'

It could be said that the FA's ban, trying to stop women from playing football, was a failure. They had succeeded in preventing them from playing on league grounds, but the never-say-die attitude of the ladies was quite remarkable, and their spirit could not be broken. They would play anywhere they could and the crowds still turned up in their thousands to watch them. By 1923 they claimed to have raised £70,000 for charitable causes.

They did not play as often as they had in the early days, but they did continue playing, and their dogged determination to play the game they loved was a credit to them. Contrary to some reports, the team did play throughout the 1920s, but their games were now mainly played during the summer months.

After the First World War, the ladies who had been employed at Dick, Kerr's on war placings, including those who were members of the football team, were released from the factory when there was no longer a need for munitions. The men had returned from the fighting in Europe and they were resuming their place in the workforce. Consequently there were fewer jobs to be found for the ladies, and although Mr Frankland did try to find work for all the team members at the factory, this was not always possible. Frenchwoman Carmen Pomies, for instance, worked in the offices.

There now began a long association between Whittingham Hospital and Dick, Kerr Ladies football team. Alfred Frankland was responsible for getting jobs at the hospital for many of the girls involved with the team. Whether it was Mr Frankland's direct influence, or that of his sister, who worked at the hospital as a ward sister, in getting the players a job is uncertain. Whittingham was a psychiatric hospital and the work was long and hard, and so the nurses who worked there needed to be fit and healthy. The nurses employed at Whittingham were able to live in, and this may well have made the idea of working there a more attractive proposition for members of the team. The hospital committee were very sports-minded and they did encourage those who were actively involved in playing all kinds of sport. Quite a number of those involved with the football team also represented Whittingham in the hospital cricket and hockey teams. Some of the players known to have worked at the hospital in the early days of the football team were Florrie Redford, Lily Lee, Jessie Walmsley, Lily Parr, Lizzy Ashcroft, Lydia Ackers, Eva Gardner and Lily Martin.

Lydia Ackers remembers, 'Mr Frankland got me my job at Whittingham; he was in with everybody. After the war there was no work at Dick, Kerr's and when the team were finishing at the factory, they all went to work at the hospital. I worked there for thirty-two years.'

In the summer of 1925, the French Ladies made yet another of their regular trips to England, where they played a series of nine matches with Dick, Kerr Ladies. News of the trip travelled as far afield as Australia, when on 19 June 1925, the *Brisbane Courier* published a photograph of the two teams lining up before the kick-off.

Some time during 1926, something rather disturbing happened at the Dick, Kerr works which raises yet more questions about the management of the club. Alice Norris says, 'Dick, Kerr's stopped us from playing on Ashton Park. There was some trouble because one day, while we were working, someone said that we all [the team] had to meet in the watch house. Something must have gone wrong because it was all so sudden that afternoon at the works. It was our training night and we were told not to go up to Ashton Park any more. Something must have gone wrong between him [Mr Frankland] and the firm. I don't know what it was, but the girls didn't come in to work the morning after, they all went with Mr Frankland. He knew he had a place where the girls could go to keep them all together'.

'When they all left, Mr Frankland was still calling the team Dick, Kerr Ladies for a while, but one of the workmen said he had heard that he hadn't to use the name Dick, Kerr's any more, so they changed their name to Preston Ladies, but Mr Frankland was always with them. I didn't go with them when they left the works, I wasn't giving up my job. Mr Frankland wanted me to take over as the physiotherapist and he said he would pay for me to learn the job properly, but my father said I hadn't to go.'

Alice went on, 'There was one time when we were playing up in Scotland and two players from the other team told us that we would not be asked back again as we were too expensive. We didn't really understand what they meant, because we were only given what it had cost us to get there. I think that's when all the trouble must have started down at the works.'

We can only guess as to what this 'trouble' at the works was really all about, and the truth will now never be known, but it must have been serious. What really made all these people leave? And is there any substance to Lydia Acker's claim that Ashton Park had actually been bought with the team's funds? Alfred Frankland worked in the offices at Dick, Kerr & Co. Ltd, and during his involvement with organizing the ladies' football team, he was able to buy a business in the Fulwood area of Preston. One can only speculate as to whether Alfred Frankland's intentions and involvement in women's football were as pure and honourable as he claimed.

Alice Norris recalls, 'No one could ever prove anything, but I think there was something in the rumours. The older players used to say that when Mr Frankland first came down here he didn't have two ha'pennies to rub together. There was all that kind of talk going about. And he would never let anybody take over.'

Lydia Ackers remembers: 'Well, he had a greengrocer's shop in Sharoe Green Lane and his wife used to run it. He was a good manager, but we had a bit of difficulty getting our expenses from him. He would try to get away with it if he could, but I wouldn't let him. I used to say, "We want paying or we won't play." Well that did it, when we said we wouldn't play he gave us our expenses. He came to see my parents when they wanted me to play for them. He was always well dressed; of course he was looking after himself wasn't he? I think that's how he bought his fruit shop.'

Elsie Yates from Fleetwood, who began playing for the team around 1923 and continued well into the 1930s, said, 'He was awkward with the girls, you know, but I was all right so I didn't bother about him. All the money was given to him and we just got our bare expenses, what we lost through not being at work, but he was always there with his money bags. Sometimes it was hard work getting money from him.'

With the matches less frequent than before, taking place perhaps once a fortnight or once a month, some of the original members of the team turned out for them only if they were really needed, although they did keep up their involvement with the club. Alice Kell played in goal before becoming the trainer for some time before she was married. Florrie Redford emigrated to Canada to persue her career as a nurse. She did return to Lancashire in 1937 and tried to make a comeback with the team. She said she had always kept herself fit while in Canada by training with the men. Alas, her comeback, although well reported in the press, was to last for only one match, the new players, being younger and benefiting from playing regular games, keeping her out of the team. Jennie Harris continued playing into the early 1930s, and of course Lily Parr went on to become one of the team's greatest, if not their greatest, player.

But what did it all mean to the players themselves? Did they realize just how important their contribution and achievements would be to the history of women's football? How did they feel about playing football and the opportunities it brought for them?

Elsie Yates, born in 1902, played right-half for the team. She recalls, 'I don't think there is a place in England where we didn't play. I enjoyed all the travelling and the good times we had. We always had big crowds wherever we played. They were good days; I really did enjoy myself.'

Elsie worked at Dick, Kerr's for a time before returning to her home town of Fleetwood, where she worked in the fish industry. 'I used to get time off work as easy as anything when I was playing football,' she said. Elsie lived in Fleetwood in a residential home for the elderly until her death in 1995. She was ninety-two years old.

Alice Norris said of playing on First Division grounds in front of all the big crowds, 'We just took it all in our stride, but it was a terrible shock when the FA stopped us from playing on their grounds. We were all very upset but we ignored them when they said that football wasn't a suitable game for ladies to play.'

Lydia Ackers, a nippy little midfield player, said her fondest memories were 'the travelling and staying in the different hotels. When we went to London we would stay where all the business people stayed and we were always very well treated.'

Asked what she remembered about the players in the team, Lydia said, 'Well, you see, I was so young. They were famous and everybody made such a fuss of them. I really had this feeling of inferiority about the likes of Florrie Redford, and her being centre-forward in this great team.' And she said of Lily Parr, 'I have never seen any woman, nor many a man, kick a ball like she could. Everybody was amazed when they saw her power; you would never believe it.'

Throughout this transitional period for the Dick, Kerr team, the public were always willing spectators at their matches, and to dispel the 'novelty' myth which has followed the women's game since its inception, it is instructive to hear the opinion of eighty-year-old William Crook, from Preston. Mr Crook saw Dick, Kerr's play on several occasions just before the General Strike of 1926. He said that like many other people he went along to see them because he enjoyed watching a good game of football, and 'Dick, Kerr Ladies had some brilliant players'.

Their extremely high standards were still firmly set, but could their phenomenal success story continue despite all the obstacles that had been placed before them? Could their reputation as the best in the world remain intact in their new guise as Preston Ladies, and if so, how long would it last?

7 Preston Ladies (the World-famous Dick, Kerr's)

Although they had now adopted their new name of Preston Ladies, the team would continue to be known as Dick, Kerr Ladies throughout their playing years, right up to the present day.

New players who joined the team in 1926, becoming household names in the second generation of the club, were Edith Hutton, Sue Chorley and Polly Scott. They were regular members of the team for at least ten years or more. Also in 1926, the team played in another night match at Burnley, employing the same kind of lighting technique used at Deepdale six years earlier. It was said that the ground was so well illuminated that a *Lancashire Daily Post* reporter was able to read the *Football Post* in the centre of the field!

By 1927 the team were still rated the best in the country and, on 8 September, in a match played at Leicester against Blackpool Ladies, the Preston side notched up a convincing 11–2 victory. The headline in the *Leicester Mercury* was: 'WOMEN CAN PLAY FOOTBALL'. The article went on:

> Everyone who went to the game came away with one big impression. And that was that they had seen an outside-left (Lily Parr) who if she had been a man would have gained international honours. She really was extraordinarily good and she scored five of her side's eleven goals. She made wing play look absurdly simple and there is no doubt that this girl has a natural ability for the game. The Dick, Kerr eleven were far too good for the Blackpool girls and whoever has coached them has done his work well, for they displayed a knowledge of the game and revealed skill that was surprising. The Dick, Kerr team was: J. Frankland, P. Scott, L. Ashcroft, E. Buxton, F. Redford, E. Latham, H. Parkinson,

J. Harris, L. Buxton, H. Shaw, L. Parr. Jennie Harris, Lily Parr and Flo Redford being the only survivors of the 'old guard'.

A story which illustrates the kind of fun they had, and typifies Lily Parr's sense of humour, comes out in this amusing little tale.

It was at a time when it was fashionable to wear straw boaters. The team were travelling home on the coach late one night, and after their usual merrymaking, some of the girls wanted to 'spend a penny'. The driver pulled up by a wall which, unbeknownst to anyone, was a reservoir. Jennie Harris, being the most desperate for the toilet, leapt over the wall in the dark, quickly followed by Lily Parr, while most of the others were still half asleep on the bus. After a few minutes, Lily strolled back on to the bus, in her own inimitable way, and said, 'Oi, thy lot, wake up. Can any of you swim?' When asked why she replied, 'Well, there's a bloody hat floating about out there and I can't see Jennie Harris underneath it!'

The French Ladies' regular visit to play a series of charity matches had evolved into a tour solely with the Dick, Kerr team. This may have been partly due to a shortage of other women's teams as opposition, coupled with the pulling power of the famous Dick, Kerr name. The players would arrange to take their two weeks' summer holiday for the tour, and both teams would travel up and down the country raising money for charity. It shows the depth of their dedication, in that year after year, they would all give up their holidays with family and friends to help deserving causes through playing football.

The Wall Street Crash of 1929 saw millions of dollars wiped off the New York Stock Exchange, and the effects of this were a contributing factor to the worldwide depression of the 1930s, which was to last for the greater part of the decade. In 1931 the depression deepened, and the great financial crisis began to take hold as the bank rate fell. There was a serious weakening in sterling and in British funds, and by the end of the year it was announced by the government that owing to the prevailing depression, and the need for economy, work on the Cunard ship '534' would have to be suspended. It would be two years before work would be resumed on the 534 which, when launched, was christened the *Queen Mary*.

Other world events at the start of the new decade saw Amy Johnson make her solo flight to Australia in just under three weeks, and the world was shocked by the wreck of the airship R101 during a storm at Beauvais in France. The airship struck a hillside, exploded and burst into flames. Only six out of a total of fifty-four crew and passengers were saved. This disaster resulted in the abandonment of all airship construction by Great Britain.

In November 1930, the *Daily Dispatch* reported that Mr Frankland had received a letter from Prague inviting him to send out two teams to play in exhibition games in Czechoslovakia. Presumably the funds were not available to make this trip, though, as it never came to fruition.

Preston Ladies were still in great demand for their fund-raising efforts, however, and they were glad to be of service in yet another time of crisis for those in need. A major signing for them in 1931 was that of Margaret Thornborough. She was the sister of Eli Thornborough, who played half-back for Bolton Wanderers and Preston North End. Margaret would in later years become the assistant manager of Preston Ladies with Alfred Frankland.

In December of 1932 the team was invited to play a game against Lovell's Ladies at Newport, south Wales, in aid of the Mayor's Christmas Distress Fund. The match was to take place at Newport Athletic Rugby Ground arena, and was to be played at night under floodlights. In those days, football by floodlight was an attraction in itself, and it is quite probable that this game was the first played by women under floodlit conditions. It was certainly only the second time that a floodlit match had been played in Newport.

The Lovell's team was made up of young ladies, all of whom were under seventeen years of age. They were a relatively inexperienced side but were unbeaten in their matches before taking on the might of Preston Ladies.

After travelling by road through the night, Dick, Kerr's arrived in Newport at approximately nine o'clock, and were met by the mayor's secretary. Despite the long overnight journey they seemed quite refreshed after having breakfast at the Queens Hotel. At ten o'clock they went to the town hall, where they were cordially welcomed at a civic reception given for them by the mayor, Councillor Mr W. J. Wall, who expressed his deep appreciation at their kindness in assisting his distress fund. Times were difficult, and he had a big task in front of him in trying to relieve the distress in Newport. During the afternoon, the Preston team were shown around the Lovell's works.

A crowd of 7,000 came along to Newport Rugby Ground on 8 December 1932, to see history in the making as women's football passed another landmark by playing at night under floodlights.

Royal Lancashire Show, 1932.
Lizzy 'Tommy' Ashcroft (on left) going for goal.

THE FAMOUS PRESTON LADIES' F.C., Late DICK KERR LADIES' F.C.
THE UNDISPUTED WORLD'S CHAMPIONS WHO HAVE TOURED EXTENSIVELY ABROAD
WINNERS OF 8 SILVER CUPS AND 4 SETS OF GOLD MEDALS

Team Postcard, 1932.
Back row (left to right): Lizzy Ashcroft, Miss Hodgkinson, Elsie
Yates, Maggie Shaw, Lily Buxton, Miss Knowles, Edna Clayton.
Middle row (left to right): Annie Yates, Lydia Ackers, Jennie
Harris, Mr. Frankland, Lily Parr, Sue Chorley, Edith Hutton.
Front row (seated on floor left to right) Hilda Parkinson,
Margaret Thornborough.

The Preston team was: Annie Derbyshire, Edna Clayton, Lizzy Ashcroft, Lily Buxton, Edith Hutton, Polly Scott, Lydia Ackers, Margaret Thornborough, Sue Chorley, Hilda Parkinson, Lily Parr.

Preston were easily the superior side, recording a convincing 5–0 victory with goals scored by Buxton, Parr, Hutton, Thornborough and Chorley. After the game, the *Daily Dispatch* reported that the Lovell's captain had conceded: 'Dick, Kerr's were a bit too good for us', and Lily Parr, the Preston captain, said; 'I would have liked them to score a goal', attributing her team's victory to the lack of experience of their opponents. After the match, both teams were entertained to a dinner and dance by the mayor at the King's Head Hotel.

Towards the end of 1933, Mr Frankland received a letter from a Belgian team, Atalante Ladies from Brussels. They had heard of the Dick, Kerr success story and wanted to play them, as they themselves were unbeaten during the last three years. A series of matches was arranged, to be played in the summer of 1934. Atalante Ladies caused something of a sensation when they beat the Preston team at Bolton, but this was to be their only victory of the tour.

The same year was also a good one for British tennis: for the first time ever, Great Britain scored two remarkable successes at Wimbledon. Dorothy Round won the women's singles, and Fred Perry won the first of his three successive singles titles. It was also the year that saw the opening of the Mersey Tunnel by King George V.

Plans were on the table for another trip to France for Dick, Kerr Ladies, and in April of 1935 they crossed the Channel to play a series of matches. It was the team's first visit since they had played there some fifteen years earlier, in 1920, and it was to prove to be their last trip abroad. As they were leaving, the Mayor of Preston gave them some white heather to bring them luck on the tour. On this trip, none of the party suffered from seasickness on the night crossing, and during the voyage the Band of the Scots Guards, who were en route to Montpellier to fulfil an engagement, entertained the passengers by playing some musical selections.

The team had one or two disappointments in their game in Paris. Apart from losing the game by 5–2, they had to play in red jerseys for the first time because of a colour clash, and they also had to play with three reserves. On their jerseys, they wore the white heather given to them by the mayor, but there was no luck going their way in this game. It was a big shock for them to lose to the

French Ladies. Perhaps the absence of Lily Parr in this game was a significant factor, and the goalkeeper, making her debut for Dick, Kerr's, found the occasion a little too much in front of the large crowd. The team was: Bessie Cunliffe, Edna Clayton, Lizzy Ashcroft, Miss Donoghue, Lily Buxton, Polly Scott, Sue Chorley, Margaret Thornborough, Edith Hutton, Hilda Parkinson, Annie Lynch.

In July, the French team were back in Preston once again. The regularity of their visits must surely prove that there was a place for women's football; it is difficult enough in modern times to attract continental teams to play football in England. The fact that it was an annual event in times when travel was a lot more time-consuming merely confirms that the women's game was flourishing.

In 1936, English Electric sold the Ashton Park site to Preston Borough Council for £27,500. They did this to help finance production at the firm as they switched from making trams and buses to manufacturing Hampden bombers. Locally, work was in progress to build the Royal Ordnance Factory at Euxton, and Courtauld's was being built to produce rayon for parachutes and barrage balloons. The opening of these two factories was considerably to ease unemployment problems in Preston.

It had always been a custom within women's football to have a famous celebrity at their matches to kick off the game. For the French visit in August of 1937, the well-known comedian George Formby, and his wife Beryl, were invited along to do the honours for the international match at Bolton. Gracie Fields was another big name to kick off for them.

The club had now been in existence for twenty years, and throughout this period had proved time and time again that they were the best women's football team in the world. They had maintained their high standards with each new generation of the team, consistently producing a fine blend of extremely talented and skilful players, and girls from all over the country still wanted to play for Dick, Kerr Ladies. They therefore felt more than justified in calling themselves world champions, but there were, of course, others who had different ideas.

Such a team was to be found in Edinburgh, and a challenge was offered to Dick, Kerr Ladies by Mrs Proctor, the secretary of the Scottish team, who had seen the official headed paper of the Preston team which had printed on it in bold black letters, 'CHAMPIONS OF THE WORLD'. Of course they claimed this title because of their impressive playing record, and because they had defeated representative sides from other European countries.

The girls from Edinburgh, however, disputed their right to call themselves the champions of the world, given that Preston's Ladies had not played them, the best team in Scotland. The challenge was promptly accepted by the team and the match was arranged to take place at the Squires Gate Stadium, South Shore, Blackpool.

Although they felt confident that no other women's team in the world were their equals, Mr Frankland said the team should undergo intensive training in preparation for the game, which was quickly reported by most of the newspapers as a world championship match. The *Daily Mail, Daily Herald, Daily Sketch, Lancashire Daily Post, Daily Mirror, Daily Express* and the *Daily Dispatch* were all keen to photograph the Preston team in training, and Mrs Patricia Moores from Liverpool, the President of the English Ladies' Hockey Leagues Association, agreed to present gold medals to the winners.

In the build-up to the match, Mr Frankland said in the *Daily Mail* of 30 August 1937:

> We are told that the Scottish lasses have beaten two men's teams and consider their craft will overcome the speed of the English team. But we have no fear on that score. Never since Preston began its brilliant history in women's football have they come across a team in Great Britain, France, Belgium, or America whom we have not beaten. We are going out for a big victory. I believe that the present Preston forward line is the best ever seen in women's football, and I am certain that we shall win. I admit there has never actually been a world championship, but when you consider all the foreign teams we have defeated, I think we are entitled to call ourselves World Champions.

The Preston side had a better record than their opponents. They had already won all of their twenty-six matches that year, while the Edinburgh girls had won eighteen, drawn one and lost one. They were the first Scottish girls' team to cross the border.

The Lancashire lasses therefore started the match as favourites and Mr Frankland was confident of a Preston victory: 'I'll eat my hat if we don't win,' he said. And as he wore outsize hats, one could not fault his confidence. 'Everybody says we are the world champions, except Edinburgh that is. But they will acknowledge it after the game.' Daphne Coupe, centre-half for Preston, said: 'The match will be a big test for us,' and May Helme, the goalkeeper, added, 'We are regarding this as our biggest match. Our season is nearly over now, as we play largely in the summer, but we are always ready to take up a challenge.' The night before the match, the team was gathered at the home of Mr Frankland (known as 'Pop' to the girls) to discuss tactics and plan their strategy for the game. The girls were taking this match more seriously than any other.

On Wednesday 8 September 1937, Preston Ladies played Edinburgh Ladies for the championship of Great Britain and the world. The team was: May Helme, Margaret Thornborough, Lucy Hoyle, Hilda Parkinson, Daphne Coupe, Sue Chorley, Joan Whalley, Irene Phillips, Edith Hutton (captain), Annie Lynch, Lily Parr.

Both sides were used to gates averaging 5,000, but only one thousand spectators – a small crowd by their standards, especially for a game given such a high profile – turned up to watch the match at Squires Gate. They saw a hard-fought contest resulting in a 5–1 victory for the Preston girls.

All the Preston goals were scored in the first half, as the home side took full advantage of the weather conditions. Having won the toss, they decided to play with a strong breeze at their backs. A hat-trick was scored by centre-forward Edith 'Ginger' Hutton. The other goals came from Lily Parr and Joan Whalley, who at fifteen was the youngest player on the field. It was said again that had Lily Parr been a male footballer, she would undoubtedly have been an international. She was prominent for the Preston team, and her strength of shot was always a problem for the Scottish side. The Edinburgh goal was scored by Frances Macdonald, who flashed through the Preston defence to score a fine goal. Mrs Macdonald said after the match, 'We were well beaten, but it was a good game and we shall play Preston again.'

Joan Whalley had taken the day off school to play in the most important match of her first season with the team. After the game someone put a mouth organ in her hand, she smiled and immediately began playing lively tunes which cheered up the tired players from both teams. It demonstrated their good sportsmanship, and their respect for one another, as they all joined in the post-match sing-song. To celebrate their victory and the twentieth anniversary of the club's formation, a World's Championship Victory Dinner was held at Booth's Café in Preston

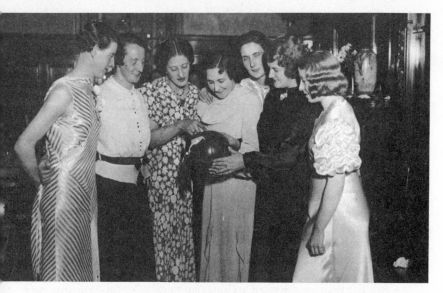

At the celebration dinner, 1937 with a ball from the USA tour
in 1922 given to them by President Harding.
Left to right: Lucy Hoyle, Edith Hutton, Margaret
Thornborough, May Helme, Lily Parr, Alice Kell, Joan Whalley.

Table card for 1937 World's Championship Victory Dinner
at Booth's Café.

Preston Ladies' Football Team
1937.

—

Goal :
M. E. Helme

Right Back :   *Left Back :*
M. A. Thornborough   L. Hoyle

Right Half :   *Centre Half :*   *Left Half :*
H. Parkinson   D. M. Coupe   S. Chorley

Right Wing :   *Centre :*   *Left Wing :*
J. Whalley   I. Phillips   E. T. Hutton   A. Lynch   L. Parr

Reserve :
S. Briggs.

—

Hon. Sec. and Manager :
A. Frankland

Preston Ladies' Football Club
1917—1937.

WORLD'S CHAMPIONSHIP

Victory
Dinner

at Booth's Cafe,
Preston.

—

Presided over by
Capt. E. C. Cobb, D.S.O., M.P.

—

Wednesday, November 24th, 1937,
at 7-30 p.m.

Championship Victory Dinner was held at Booth's Café in Preston on 24 November 1937.

On the menu was a choice of tomato cocktail or grapefruit starters, celery soup, lemon sole and tartar sauce, roast chicken and sausage, baked and boiled potatoes, sprouts and peas, followed by plum pudding and sauce or apple tart and cream, and finally, coffee. The tables were decorated in the club's colours of black and white, and prominently displayed were bannerettes won by the team when playing against teams in America, France and Canada, and the visiting team from Belgium.

Among the many dignitaries present at the dinner, given by Sir Meyrick Hollins, were Captain Cobb, MP for Preston, Mrs Pat Moores and Alderman Mrs A. M. Pimblett, and the proceedings were well reported in the *Lancashire Daily Post*, *Daily Dispatch*, *Daily Herald* and *Daily Mail* on 25 November 1937. The guest of honour for the team was Mrs Alice Cook, formerly Alice Kell, the first ever captain of the famous Dick, Kerr team in their inaugural 1917 season. She expressed her opinion to the press before the dinner that the team she had played in was as good as the present team, which was maintaining the standards established by the older brigade. The original captain modestly said nothing about her own part, but she had had few equals as a full-back.

Edith Hutton, the captain at the time, disagreed and thought that the current side was the finest the world had seen. 'I don't deny the brilliance of some of the former players,' she said, 'but we now have a superior balance and blend.' Miss Hutton had played for the team for eleven years and both captains agreed that they had never known any harmful results to women from playing football.

Captain Cobb paid a neat compliment to the girls by saying that he, like everyone else, had heard of this wonderful football team who had beat all of their rivals, but had imagined that ladies who played such a vigorous game would be 'pretty tough guys'. This was met with laughter from those present and he went on to say he was glad to have that illusion removed, because he now realized that women could play a 'man's' game without losing any of their femininity. The most striking thing about the club, in addition to its great achievements on the field of play, was its raising of tens of thousands of pounds for charitable purposes, which was something that must make a strong appeal to everybody. Captain Cobb proposed the toast for the team and wished the club continued success.

In replying, Mr Frankland said that since 1917 the women footballers had raised over £100,000 for various hospitals, ex-soldiers, poor children and even football and cricket clubs, without a penny for personal gain. He said that they had had many offers to go about 'stunting' for private gain, but had always turned a deaf ear to them. 'Since our inception,' he said 'we have played 437 matches, won 424, lost seven and drawn six, scored 2,863 goals and had only 207 scored against. We have raised over £100,000 in this country and in foreign lands for charity. We have won fourteen silver cups, five of them outright, and hold a trophy awarded for the most meritorious assistance given to ex-servicemen.'

For the players, speeches in reply were made by team captain Edith Hutton and vice-captain Margaret Thornborough.

In presenting the medals, Mrs Moores said she had always admired the team from afar for the help they had given to deserving causes. Alderman Mrs A. M. Pimblett recalled that when she was mayor she had the privilege of welcoming the Belgian and Preston teams at the town hall. She thought the Preston girl footballers could be proud of having helped to make the town of Preston better known in various parts of the world.

So a glittering and most memorable night held in the team's honour came to a close. This must surely have been the pinnacle of their career. They were, quite literally, the toast of the town.

Fifty-four years later, in China in 1991, the Women's World Championship for the M&Ms Cup was staged by FIFA. Women's football teams from Europe, Asia, the United States of America, Africa, South America and Oceania competed in qualifying tournaments for a place in this competition, which was also known as the first Women's World Cup.

Twelve countries went on to compete in the final rounds in this historic event. They were: China, Norway, Denmark, New Zealand, the United States of America, Sweden, Brazil, Japan, Germany, Italy, Taiwan and Nigeria. The competition was played in three groups of four with China, Germany and the USA all winning their groups to reach the quarter-finals, along with Sweden, Denmark and Taiwan.

The emergence of the United States women's national team on to the world stage, since its formation in 1985, came as no surprise to their coach Anson Dorrance. He believes that there are four parts to the game of football, technical, tactical, physical and psychological, and he teaches his players about all of them.

World Champions! Cheers!
Left to right: Stella Briggs, Mary Bowles, Lily Parr,
Joan Whalley, Bessie Cunliffe.

A thrilling semi-final saw the USA defeat Germany by 5–2, proving that they can more than hold their own with the best footballing nations in the world. In the other semi-final, Norway defeated Sweden 4–1. The final was staged at Canton, China on 30 November 1991. The USA defeated Norway 2–1 to become the winners of the first Women's World Cup.

In the opinion of Anson Dorrance, the most dominating woman player in the world is Michele Akers. The twenty-six year-old striker from Oviedo, Florida had averaged more than a goal a game for the national side since 1988, after being switched from midfield to forward by Dorrance.

Lily Parr, when playing in the World Championship match in 1937, was described by her manager, Alfred Frankland as 'the best outside-left playing in the world today', and Bobby Walker, a famous Scottish footballer, described her as 'the best natural timer of a football I have ever seen'. We can only speculate about how Michele Akers would have compared to some of those wonderful ladies who played on the world stage all those years ago. How would she have handled such defenders as Alice Kell or Jessie Walmsley? Admittedly, the level of training received in the USA today is of a high standard, but if the same opportunities could have been given to the likes of Kell, Redford, Harris and Parr, one suspects that English women's football would be in a much healthier state than it is today.

It would be interesting to go back in time and, under the same conditions as those played in the pioneering days of women's football (with the heavy leather footballs and rock-hard boots), compare the skills of the likes of Flo Redford, Jennie Harris, Lily Parr and company with those of the modern-day world champions.

It was written in the *Stalybridge Reporter* on 5 February 1921, of Lily Parr when she had just started playing football at the tender age of fourteen,

> There is probably no greater football prodigy in the whole country. Not only has she speed and excellent ball control, but her admirable physique enables her to brush off challenges from defenders who tackle her. She amazes the crowd wherever she goes by the way she swings the ball clean across the goalmouth to the opposite wing.

Joan Whalley, herself one of Dick, Kerr Ladies' all-time greats, said of Lily Parr, 'She had a kick like a mule. She was the only person I knew who could lift a dead ball, the old heavy leather ball, from the left wing over to me on the right and nearly knock me out with the force of the shot. Those old balls used to retain the wet, and the longer the game went on in wet weather, the heavier the ball became, but it never bothered Parr. When she took a left corner kick, it came over like a bullet, and if you ever hit one of those with your head... I only ever did it once and the laces on the ball left their impression on my forehead and cut it open. I thought, never again, not from one of Parr's crosses.'

The ladies taking the world stage in 1991 were probably unaware of those who had gone before them, but whatever happens in women's football, in all probability, Dick, Kerr Ladies did it first.

8 Up to World War Two

The 1938 season began in August and the French Ladies returned for a four-day tour, playing matches in the Lancashire area. In November, Flo Redford returned from Montreal, Canada, where she had been living since 1930. She had written to Mr Frankland telling him of her return and asking if they had any need of her services in the football team. Speaking in the *Daily Mirror*, he said: 'If ever there was a natural woman footballer it was Miss Redford. She was a wonderful dribbler of a ball and had a powerful shot. She helped to make the team what it is today and I shall give her a try out. If she is anything like she was, she will be given her place again.' Flo was quoted in the *Lancashire Daily Post* as saying that she was looking forward to returning to football again after her long absence, and intended to play for her old team as often as she could. She made her comeback for Preston Ladies at the age of thirty-six, playing in her former position of centre-forward against Whitehaven Ladies. She must have known in her heart, however, that she could not recapture her old form.

Opposition to women's football came to the fore once again in 1938 – although it had never really gone away – but this particular incident further illustrates the hypocrisy surrounding the game. Reported in the *Daily Mirror* on 6 December, Mr Ted Robbins, the Secretary of the Welsh FA, banned a women's charity match from taking place in Wales. 'It's a man's game and women don't look well playing it,' was Mr Robbins's statement on the matter. Mr Frankland replied, saying,

> I would very much like Mr Robbins to recall 1919 when the recently-formed Dick, Kerr Ladies played St Helens on the Wrexham racecourse. The gates had to be closed owing to the big crowd. Mr Robbins was there, with the rest of the Welsh FA officials, and they gave the Dick, Kerr team the Welsh dragon to wear on their jerseys. All the officials were delighted with the game, and afterwards Mr Robbins

93

and others handed out bouquets to the women for their fine display. It is a nonsense to suggest that football is not a women's game. At that match at Wrexham in 1919, the verdict was a unanimous one in favour of women's football so long as women played women. Women's football has been justified and has raised thousands of pounds for charity, but apparently what was OK nearly twenty years ago is just the opposite today. I cannot understand the complete changeover.

In August 1939, just before the outbreak of the Second World War, the Belgian team had returned for another tour which took in eleven matches with Dick, Kerr's. On this tour, the visitors could not emulate their famous victory of 1934, failing to win any of their games with the Preston team. Joe Loss, the famous bandleader, was another of the celebrities who came along to kick off at one of the matches.

At the time of the Belgian tour, Nancy Thomson, who played for Edinburgh Ladies, was on holiday in Preston, staying at the home of Joan Whalley. Mr Frankland was keen for Nancy to join the team as she had previously helped Edinburgh to gain a well-deserved victory over Dick, Kerr's, by scoring a hat-trick against them.

Nancy recalls, 'I was invited to be a guest player for Preston against the Belgian side and ended up staying for fifteen years! Both my parents were dead and I was living with my married sister, so I had no strong ties. She had a fit when I sent for my clothes.

'Joan's family were absolutely marvellous to me, they adopted me like one of their own, especially her mum. My mother had died when I was seven years old, and believe me I adored Joan's mother, she was wonderful. Mr Frankland had contacted me several times about playing for the team. He said a job would be found for me and also a place to live. He had a lot of influence at Whittingham Hospital and he got me a job there without any form to sign, no introduction, not even an interview. So I started working at Whittingham on the Friday before war broke out on the Sunday. The hospital were very keen on sport, and they welcomed me with open arms. I finished up playing hockey, cricket and badminton for the hospital teams, whilst other poor devils were making beds!

'At that time, Whittingham and indeed every other psychiatric hospital were all enclosed, they all had locked doors. That meant that we had to supply the entertainment for the patients from the inside, so we had a staff hockey, cricket and badminton team. We had a very extensive sports programme and once a year all the jewellers in Preston gave prizes like cigarette lighters and watches etc. It was a very big hospital with each division having its own matron and we all competed against each other. For the patients' entertainment, a nurse from each ward would take all those who were able to go out, to watch us playing cricket or hockey or whatever it was. There would be hundreds of patients all around, and they even had a "bookie" on the races!'

Nancy became an immediate regular in the Dick, Kerr team, playing at either centre-forward or centre-half, and she soon earned the nickname 'Cannonball' from her team-mates.

After spending fifteen years nursing at Whittingham Hospital, she joined the Colonial Nursing Service, and was posted to Gibraltar as 'Sister Thomson'. It was while she was on holiday in Spain that she hit the headlines for something other than, and different from, playing football.

Nancy and a friend were on the beach at Algeciras, on the south coast of Spain, when they heard cries for help. Her friend, who was in a bathing suit, dived in and swam towards a drifting dinghy which had a young mother and her two children on board. After reaching the dinghy she found she was too exhausted to push them towards the beach. It was then that Nancy, who was fully clothed, dived in and swam out to complete the rescue, bringing them all safely back to the shore.

It was during the Belgian visit that Alfred Frankland claimed to have received a telegram from the War Office asking him to make sure all the Belgian players went home after their last match on 24 August 1939. War was declared just over a week later, on 3 September 1939.

Joan Whalley remembers, 'They didn't want to go back because they were afraid. My friend Arlene said to me, "I don't want to go back. Can I stay with you and your family until the war is over?"

'They had to go back, of course, and after the war we heard about members of the team who had been raped and shot by the Germans; it was a terrible time. We heard that some Germans had gone into one of the girls' homes and tried to rape her. She struggled and fought for her life but they shot her. It was heartbreaking to hear these stories.'

The team were to play only a handful of games after the outbreak of the war, all against Bolton Ladies. In November 1939

Joan (Tich) Burke, aged 15.

Nellie Halstead, bronze medal winner at the 1936 Olympics;
Nellie wasn't a bad centre-forward either.

they played them at St Helens, where they won 9–4, and in
Leeds, where they drew 3–3. In January of 1940 they played at
Bolton and won 3–2, and in March the game was played at
Hindsford, which they drew 3–3.

There were obvious travel difficulties during the war with the
rationing of petrol and of course the air raids, so the football team
were more or less put on hold until the ending of the hostilities.
Mr Frankland was involved as an ARP (Air Raid Precautions)
warden for the duration of the war. This involved escorting
people safely to the air raid shelters when the sirens went off, and
ensuring that no lights were visible during the blackout. Mr
Ernest Hunt, the manager of Bolton Ladies, worked for a Bolton
hospital, and he organized several games between the two teams
to raise money for charities in Bolton.

The Bolton side were one of the few teams on almost the same
level as Preston Ladies, and their games were always skilful,
entertaining and close-fought contests. Their famous centre-
forward was none other than Nellie Halstead, the Olympic
sprinter, who won a bronze medal with the relay team in the 1936
Olympics. Nellie was running last and the team were lying in fifth
position when she took the baton, and as she said, 'I ran like hell,
I must have run the race of my life!'

In 1941, Mr Hunt organized a trip to Wales for Bolton and
Preston Ladies, where they played a series of five games. Another
game arranged by him, and possibly the last before the end of the
fighting, was played at Horwich, on Saturday 25 October 1941.

Even through those dreadful times of the Second World War,
there was still some kind of humour to be found, as Joan Whalley
relates: 'There were blackouts and all sorts happening when we
were playing and we had to take our gas masks with us wherever
we went. There were always three of us went around together,
myself, Joan Burke (Tich) and Stella Briggs. We had gone to bed
one night and Tich said, "I can smell gas." No one else could smell
anything but Tich insisted, "I'm not taking any chances," and she
got her gas mask out and put it on in bed! She was lying there
trying to talk to us with this muffled voice, but we couldn't tell
a word she was saying; it was so funny, we were all falling about
laughing. Finally we realized the gas mantle on the wall was
leaking after all and we sent for the hotel manager to get it fixed.
It's a good job we did because I had visions of us all being dead
the morning after. They didn't have North Sea gas in those days;
the gas was much more toxic than it is today.'

In May of 1943 it was reported that Alfred Frankland was repeatedly receiving requests from different parts of the country for the team to play matches for charity, and the girls in the services and war factories were writing to him asking to be given trials for the team. But to all requests Mr Frankland answered, 'Nothing doing at present. Try again after the war.' Although he could have raised a first-class team, he felt that it was not the time to revive the club, mainly because of travel difficulties and food rationing.

When the Allied forces had liberated Paris in 1944, Carmen Pomies wrote to tell Mr Frankland of the 'delirious joy of deliverance', at her country's liberation, and of being able to speak of football again, because 'the Germans had stopped us from playing'. Carmen was one of the heroines of the French Resistance and she said, 'Of course I was FFI (French Forces of the Interior) and I did it with all my heart and strength. I went on the barricades and fought my part.'

During the war Carmen was secretary to Renée St Cyr, the French film star, and she also worked in an office where a German officer signed passports. Without a thought for her own safety, she was able to serve the Resistance and help people escape, by securing passports for those wanted by the Gestapo.

The war ended on 8 May 1945, and it was in October that Carmen returned to Preston, where she stayed at the home of her friend, Flo Redford. She said in an interview in the *News Chronicle* on 5 October: 'English troops in Paris were always asking me when I was coming to England again. I have longed so much for this moment, I have been coming to Preston since 1920 when I was a schoolgirl.'

It was with the approval of the French Ministry of Sport and Education that she came to explore means of organizing women's international events again between France and England. She said in the *News Chronicle* and the *Lancashire Daily Post*,

> Our sport suffered terribly during the occupation. Football for women was stopped completely, but we kept on playing even though it had to be in secret. I did all I could to keep my team together. Even though the Germans stopped us playing football we played secretly. In a men's section of a tennis club, there was a field which the men, rather fearfully, allowed us to use. And so we played but not very often.

When it was suggested to her that keeping a football match secret must have been a tricky business, she laughed and said, 'Ah, but those Germans, they were slow. We played on the men's ground when they weren't looking. They would have thrown us in gaol if they had caught us.'

She had retained her membership of the Cercle Athlétique de Montrouge club in Paris, which had tried to keep sport alive during the war, and German girls used to go to the club to play hockey and tennis. It was a favourite trick to steal their clothes in their absence, leaving the frauleins to wander around in an undressed state!

Both teams would be resuming training in October of 1945, and if transport was sufficently relaxed it was hoped that they would begin playing again in the summer of 1946. Margaret Thornborough, now Mrs Farnworth, had been appointed assistant manager and helped with the arrangements.

Like many of the other players, Margaret was also a nurse at Whittingham Hospital and that was where she was to be found at eighty-two, suffering from dementia, now a patient herself. People who knew Margaret had advised me that a visit would be fruitless, as she was unable to remember anything.

I had been given an old photograph album by Tony Frankland, which used to belong to his grandfather, Alfred Frankland, and it contained quite a number of old photographs of Margaret, so I was hoping that maybe a spark from the past would help her remember something of her days with the Dick, Kerr team.

When I arrived at the hospital, Margaret was by chance walking in the corridor, and the ward sister told her I had come to talk to her about her time playing football for Dick, Kerr Ladies. She took my right arm and we walked down the corridor together to the day room. The room was full of other ladies who had little idea of who, or where, they were.

I showed her all the old photographs of herself playing football, tennis and bowls and the old team photographs of Dick, Kerr's, but sadly, there was no response. She just sat there staring, and I suppose she was not really seeing the photographs at all. But I hoped that as she sat there gazing at them, perhaps there would be a familiar scene that would trigger a memory and she would remember something from those far-off days when she had been a young woman in her prime. For a brief moment, it looked as though she was flicking through her mind like an old 'cardex' file, searching desperately through her memories trying to recall something in the photographs. Unfortunately it was not to be. Margaret's memories remained locked away for ever.

I was so sad for her, sad for her lost memories and sad for the way she was living out the end of her days. It is so very poignant to think that, having nursed so many people at Whittingham Hospital in days gone by, it was now Margaret's turn to be nursed there. She was transferred to another hospital, where she died in 1994.

9 Post-war Years

After the war, there were so many girls wanting to play for Preston (Dick, Kerr Ladies) that Alfred Frankland had enough players on the books to field two teams. They were regularly seen in training on Waverley Park and were frequently photographed by the press as they prepared for their first post-war matches. There was still a tremendous amount of interest in the club and many charities had great expectations with the team's re-formation, as they claimed to have raised £120,000 for charitable purposes since their inception.

Their first post-war match could have been regarded as a family affair, as the Preston club provided both teams for the match at Glossop Football Club, Derbyshire, on Good Friday, 19 April 1946. In fact fielding two teams was something Mr Frankland did quite often.

A warm welcome was given to the teams, and after having lunch with the officials of Glossop FC, they were 'played up to the ground' in their private coach, headed by the Glossop Military Band. The match was to be played in aid of the local Welcome Home Fund, and the committee had set the target of £100 which they hoped would be raised during the day.

Glossop Football Club had their biggest crowd in thirty years, when 5,000 people came to watch Dick, Kerr Ladies play Lancashire County Ladies. The crowd roared with approval as both teams took to the field, and the Glossop Military Band played, 'She's a Lassie from Lancashire'.

Lily Parr was becoming quite a legend as she reached yet another milestone in her illustrious career with the club in these post-war years. She was given the captaincy by Mr Frankland, who said it was a proud moment for him to see Lily on the field that day, as she had been with the team for twenty-six years. The press were reporting on the achievements Lily had made with the club, and the statistics stated that she had scored 967 goals out

The players line up for the press, before their first practice
match after the war. Waverley Park, 1945.
Left to right: Margaret Thornborough, Jean Moizer, Marion
Barker, Florence Coles, Doreen Norris, Frances Appleby, Lottie
Worrall, Marjorie Foulkes, Joan Whalley, Alma Hopkins, Joan
Wilkinson, Dorothy Whalley, Sally Kendal.

First practice match after the war, Waverley Park, 1945.
Lottie Worrall kicking the ball.

of the team's total score of 3,022, and that she had missed only five games since joining the team in 1920. She added another goal to her tally by scoring in the 3–1 victory over the County team. The other scorers were Margaret Thornborough and Nancy Thomson.

The first post-war team was: Brenda Keen, Jean Moizer, Hilda Parkinson, Sally Kendall, Margaret Thornborough, Stella Briggs, Joan Whalley, Joan Burke, Nancy Thomson, Annie Lynch, Lily Parr.

The teams were entertained to a civic reception after the game at the Norfolk Arms Hotel, where the mayor thanked all concerned in helping to raise £250 for his Welcome Home Fund. Mr Goldthorpe, President of Glossop Football Club, said, 'It has been a wonderful holiday event. I cannot recall a ladies' football team coming to Glossop before, and this has been a unique occasion in the history of the town.'

The Dick, Kerr show was back on the road at last, and in June they embarked on a three-day tour of Weymouth, where they won the Pitman Challenge Cup and Shield, by defeating Weymouth by 8–2 in the final of the competition.

Nancy Thomson remembers, 'Mr Frankland demanded nothing but the best for us, the absolute best. But he also expected the best from us in return. We weren't allowed to wear trousers anywhere in public; it wasn't done in those days. We could do what we liked on the bus when we were travelling, but we had to change back into our skirts or dresses in the bus before we met any of the officials – that was a must.'

Born in 1882, Alfred Frankland was typically Victorian in his values, and he would always lift his hat to the ladies. He always wore a three-piece suit, had the habit of frequently taking his watch out of his waistcoat pocket to look at the time, and he walked with a silver-topped cane. He was known as 'Father' or 'Pop' Frankland by the girls, and they often used to get the better of him when staying longer than he would wish at 'watering holes' on return journeys from away matches. At his home he had a big wooden chest full of football boots, and any new player who did not have her own boots could look through them to find a suitable pair. He was strict in his organization of the football team, as this letter, sent to each player for the Glossop match, illustrates.

In October of 1946 the Bolton Ladies manager was organizing an international match between England and Scotland at Salford Rugby Ground, and he had invited three of the Preston players

Alfred Frankland

Dear *Miss Foulkes*

Glossop Arrangements for Good Friday next.

Preston Players arrange to meet me at Moor Park Avenue, Garstang Road, Preston, at 9.0. a.m. prompt. Please be most particular to have all your football gear in very clean condition, boots and laces, etc. Most important to all players is to have their football studs examined; already in our practise games, damage has been done by nails protruding below leather of studs. Do please pay strict attention to this important detail. I shall, most probably, go around and examine all boots for any defects.

A few more points for our post-war programme :-

(i)   Be punctual in your appointments.

(ii) Always conduct yourself in such manner that will bring credit to the famous club you belong to, both on and off the field.

(iii) Reserves must have full gear exactly the same as if playing.

(iv) Certain players in the county teams will be picked up at Bolton and Manchester.

(v)   I once more appeal to all of you to give all the help you can to Mrs. Farnworth in her new appointment as Assistant Manager.

(vi) In conclusion, I wish to thank all our old players who have given up so much time in assisting to train our young players.

(vii) We all extend to Miss Parr a special welcome, and best wishes in this post-war period of her appearances with us.

Yours sincerely,

Frankland

Hon. Manager.

This letter from Frankland illustrates
his strictness with the players.

to play in the game, to take place on Sunday 17 November. Jean Moizer, Daphne Coupe and Joan Whalley were selected to play in the England team.

In a letter written to each of the players, Mr Hunt said,

> This may not meet with the approval of your manager, but if he objects to any of your players taking part, I am afraid he is not showing the sporting spirit which is necessary. No matter what little differences we may have, I can assure you it is not with you the players, for I hold every one of you in the highest esteem and I know my players do likewise.

Mr Frankland did indeed reject the invitation for the girls to play in the match, which was in aid of the Mayor's Distress Fund, because he said it was against their principle to play football on a Sunday. He stated, 'We have never played on Sunday, and we do not intend to do so, but we do of course recognise the very worthy object of the game.' Perhaps it had escaped Mr Frankland's memory that the team did in fact play on a Sunday during their visit to France in 1920.

The French team returned to Preston in June 1947, when they played five matches in eight days. It was their first visit in ten years. Mr Frankland and Margaret Thornborough said in a match programme that they did not feel that the team were quite up to their pre-war standard, but they were confident that by patient team building, they would more than hold their own with any other ladies' team. They were proud to put on record that the club had been given 159 civic receptions since their formation, including those by the Lord Mayors of London, York, Manchester, Liverpool, Sheffield, Birmingham, Belfast and Glasgow.

In 1947 the FA once again showed their pompous bigotry when a referee, Mr E. Turner, was suspended by the Kent County FA because he refused to end his association as manager/trainer with Kent Ladies FC. The Kent County Football Association were of the opinion that 'women's football brings the game into disrepute'. A newspaper clipping in Joan Whalley's scrapbook noted that, Mr Turner, an ex-RAF corporal, intended to stay with the club and said: 'All these girls are doing is what in war times would have been classed as a man's job. Where would the country be now if the powers that be had said, "That is a man's job and girls must not do it – they might bring the country into disrepute"?'

In the same year, the FA also came in for some sharp criticism from the Mayor of Stalybridge after Dick, Kerr's had played Bolton

Ladies in aid of the War Memorial Fund. Commenting on the 'arrogant and old-fashioned outlook of the FA', he said how much he appreciated their coming and playing in Stalybridge, and added, 'I hope you will go ahead and fight the FA, which is a narrow, bigoted authority. From one who has been involved in the game for thirty years, I personally resent it. Anything I can do to help you break down the barrier, I will do so.' At this time there were seventeen ladies' teams throughout the country.

The team were playing regularly in the late 1940s and were still winning most of their matches. Edna Broughton from Crewe, Alice Hargreaves from Blackpool and Jean Dent from Preston were notable signings for them. But, as before the war, Bolton Ladies were proving tough opposition and were the victors on some of their meetings.

Mr Frankland often referred to Edna Broughton as 'his little star', and in a letter to Edna's parents in September of 1947, he said:

> I wish with all my heart to say thank you for Edna. She had great promise when she came to us. But do you agree she is 100 per cent better and she will make one of the loveliest players the ladies' game has ever seen? She had Bolton on toast is spite of their fouls on her. One foul against her in the first ten minutes should have seen the Bolton right-half off the field. I love to watch her bewilder players.

Both Lily Parr and Margaret Thornborough were still playing and still scoring goals, and Lily would even play in goal if she was needed. With Margaret being the assistant manager, she played only in an emergency. Irene Swift, the daughter of Frank Swift, the England and Manchester City player, signed for the Preston team in 1949, to play in goal like her father, although she did not stay with the team long.

In June 1949 they played Blackpool Ladies at Freckleton in aid of the Village School Fund. Mr Frankland was a former resident of Freckleton and attended the school there. Before the game the team laid a wreath of thirty-eight red roses on a memorial grave in the churchyard, for the thirty-eight school children who lost their lives when an American Liberator crashed during a thunderstorm and destroyed part of the school in August 1944. Appropriately, at this simple ceremony, two members of the WRAF, both members of the Preston team, stood in salute, one at each side of the grave, while relatives of the children gathered round.

Edna Broughton, aged seventeen.

The fifth anniversary of the Freckleton air disaster, when thirty-eight children were killed by an American bomber, crash-landing on their school. In the photo Alfred Frankland is laying a wreath. The two WRAF women are Mary Carter and Doreen Richards, who both played for the team.

It was Blackpool Ladies' first game, and although they tried hard, the result was a convincing 8–1 victory for Dick, Kerr's.

The French team came over again in 1949 for another tour. They were never as good as the pre-war team and were always beaten by Dick, Kerr's, but the crowds still turned up in their thousands to watch them play. For these international matches, the Preston team were representing England, as had been the case throughout their history.

By 1950 Lily Parr, now forty-five, was playing at left-back and still getting good reviews in the press. In a 1–1 draw with Manchester Ladies at Belle Vue, a report said, 'Lily Parr was dominant at left full back. But for her long experience and positional play, Manchester might have won comfortably.' The Preston side were not outplayed, but the Manchester team did have an advantage: they practised regularly, whereas the Preston players, through living in various parts of Lancashire, never got this opportunity. It was a far cry from the days of Alice Kell, Flo Redford *et al.*

This was the first time the Preston side had been forced to advertise for players, and unless more new talent could be introduced, their impressive record would begin to have some blemishes on it.

A major signing this year was that of fifteen-year-old Jean Lane from Wigan. Kath Latham was also a new signing, and she soon began dealing with all the team's clerical work. 'Pop' had asked her to take over some of the secretarial duties of the club, as she was a competent shorthand typist. She gradually did more and more of the paperwork and as Mr Frankland's health began to fail, Kath stopped playing and became his assistant.

During the French tour of 1950, both teams travelled to Ireland to play a series of matches. The highlight of their visit was a meeting with the Queen (now the Queen Mother) during her tour of Northern Ireland. At a relatively isolated spot on her route, just outside Dunmurry, the Queen noticed a group of girls displaying an outsize French tricolour. On the Queen's instruction, the car, which had been gathering speed on an empty road, was slowed down while she gave a special greeting to both teams. They were all thrilled at this unexpected meeting with royalty.

Margaret Thornborough was to score her last goal for Dick, Kerr Ladies in a 3–1 victory against the French team at Bolton on 22 July 1950. Lily Parr's last goal for club and country was against

'Half time', 1949.
Left to right: Edna Broughton, Margaret Thornborough, Nancy Thomson, Betty Sharples, Stella Briggs, Lily Parr, Joan Whalley, unknown, Joan Burke. Lily Parr was renowned for her dressing room banter.

Joan Whalley introducing the Lord Mayor of Leeds
to the team, 1950.

Scotland at Carlisle on 12 August. She scored from the penalty spot in an 11–1 victory over the Scots.

By October of 1950, Mr Frankland calculated their record to date as played 643, won 607, drawn twenty-seven and lost only nine since 1917. He also claimed that they had raised £140,000 for charity. They ended the 1950 season unbeaten, having won all their games except for the 1–1 draw with Manchester, and Joan Burke (Tich) was the leading goalscorer, with twenty-two goals.

By 1951 there were twenty-six women's football teams in the country, and this was to be Lily Parr's last season with the Preston team. In recognition of her long and distinguished playing career, she was made an honorary life member of the club. Only Alice Kell and Margaret Thornborough had previously received this honour. Mr Frankland placed an advert in the *Lancashire Daily Post* for new players. The last few years had seen the loss of some of the longest-serving members of the team and they would prove difficult, if not impossible, to replace.

Lily Parr, especially, had played a huge part in the history of the team. It must have been a sad day for both her and Preston Ladies when she finally hung up her boots. She was the last playing link from the glory days of women's football, when they were welcome at any stadium in the country. Lily must have scored somewhere in the region of 1,000 goals for Dick, Kerr Ladies, which must make her the leading goalscorer in the club's entire history, if not the all-time leading goalscorer in women's football. As a full-back, she always said that she did not need to do a lot of running, as she knew what her opponent was going to do with the ball before she got it. She had the knack of being in the right place at the right time, and could always be relied upon to make a good defensive clearance.

Other new players in the early 1950s were June Gregson, Muriel Heaney and Audrey Coupe from Preston, Yvonne Hamer from Crewe and Joan Clay from Liverpool. Years later, Joan recalled, 'My first memory of Dick, Kerr Ladies was when I played for Littlewood's and we offered Dick, Kerr's a challenge, thinking that we were going to be the only team ever to beat them. I was very disappointed on that occasion; we lost 15–1! It was a match of mixed emotions, disappointment at losing, but admiration for the quality of play shown to us that evening by Dick, Kerr's. I joined them not long after that, and it was a truely marvellous experience playing for them.'

Preston team in 1950.
Back (left to right): Margaret Thornborough,
Betty Sharples, Lily Parr, Joan Burke, Sheila Pinder,
Nancy Thomson, Stella Briggs, Alfred Frankland.
Front (left to right): Doreen Richards, Jean Lane,
Joan Whalley, Alice Hargreaves, Barbara Gilbert.

Nancy Thomson, (left front) captain of Dick Kerr's is greeted on the pitch by (left to right) unknown, Joe McCall (ex Preston North End player), PNE and England international Tom Finney, Alfred Frankland, unknown, the captain of the Lancashire County Ladies, 1952.

Kirkham, 1952. The crowds are still there.
Back (left to right): Betty Sharples, Jean Dent, Nancy Thomson,
Margaret Goodenson, Audrey Coupe, Muriel Heaney.
Front (left to right): Joan Whalley, Joan Burke, Doreen
Richards, Jean Lane, Yvonne Hamer.

The 1952 season saw the team unbeaten for the third successive year, with Joan Burke the leading goalscorer, also for the third successive season. In this year the town of Preston celebrated the Guild. The unique Preston Guild celebrations, which occur only once every twenty years, should have taken place in 1942, but they had had to be postponed until after the war.

Alice Mills (now Mrs Lambert), who had made the trip with Dick, Kerr Ladies to the United States in 1922, and eventually settled in Seekonck, Massachusetts, returned to Preston for the Guild celebrations. She had, during her twenty-seven years of married life, raised six healthy daughters, proving that no harm came to any of the women who played football before the FA ban in 1921. And Lily Jones (now Mrs Martin) was also to see her old team in action. She too had travelled with them to the USA and France in the early 1920s.

In 1953 they were to play another match under floodlights, when they met Manchester Ladies at the vast Odsal Rugby League Stadium at Bradford. The result was a 6–2 victory for the Preston team, with Jean Lane scoring her first hat-trick for the club. Statistics at the end of the season were played 704, won 664, drawn thirty-one and lost only nine in thirty-six years.

This was also the year that Joan Whalley left Dick, Kerr's and signed for Manchester Ladies in the 1953 season, after sixteen years with the club. The reason for this shock transfer was that Joan was working for Ribble Buses as a conductress, doing split shifts. The team were due to go on tour for two weeks with the French team, and Joan had arranged her holidays accordingly. The day before they were all due to leave she had to work a late shift and did not get to bed until one in the morning. She had to be up at five to be in time to meet everyone at the hotel where the French team were staying, but that morning she overslept. She was only about twenty minutes late when she arrived at the meeting place, but they had gone without her.

Joan recalls, 'I thought they would still be there when I arrived, but there was no sign of them. They must have gone exactly on time because old Frankland was always in and out of his pocket looking at his watch. I've known times when we waited quarter of an hour for people to arrive, yet he wouldn't wait for me. I never got over it; it broke my heart. I knew they would be going through Ormskirk, and wondered if I should get on a bus to see if I could meet up with them, but I was so upset, I had a big lump in my throat and I was crying. I'd never missed a match since I started playing for Dick, Kerr's in 1937.

I went home and cried my eyes out, I never went out for the rest of that day. The next day I went to work and told them what had happened. I was crying in the office as I explained to the boss that I couldn't stay at home for two weeks knowing that they were all playing football. I asked if I could cancel my holidays and come back to work. He said I could and I started work straight away.

'When they came back, Tich came up to see me and I told her all about it, and she said, "He wouldn't wait Joan, we were on at him but he wouldn't wait."

'I thought it was disgusting. I saw him afterwards but he never apologized to me. We did speak again, though, and whenever I saw him I would always say "Hello Pop".'

Joan did return to Dick, Kerr Ladies after five years with the Manchester team, but not until after the death of 'Pop' Frankland. She played in the 1958 and 1959 seasons.

In 1955 they went on tour with a team from the Netherlands. It was the first time that a women's team from the Netherlands had ever played in England. They played a series of seven games and the Preston team were the victors on each occasion. They scored thirty-three goals during the tour, and conceded only nine. The scorers were, Jean Lane (twelve), Edna Broughton (eight), Joan Hall (seven), Alice Walmsley (two), Joan Clay (two), Joan Burke (one) and Barbara Widdows (one). Jean Lane said of the Dutch visitors, 'They were a very sporting team. In one game we had with them, one of our girls went off injured, which meant we were down to ten players. They immediately let one of their players leave the field so that they didn't have an advantage over us.'

By the end of 1955 'Pop' became ill and Kath Latham was called upon to act as manager. Kath had been doing most of the paperwork for the club since the early 1950s, and she seemed to be the obvious choice to take on the responsibility. By February of 1956 he had become very ill, so Kath and team captain Stella Briggs became joint acting managers because 'Pop' was no longer fit to travel. A week before their first match that year, he had a relapse and Kath made all the arrangements for the start of the new season.

In 1956, in a match against Manchester Ladies played at Hesketh Bank, Kath invited Alice Cook, formerly Alice Kell, the team's first ever captain, to kick off the game. It must have been quite an

emotional day for Alice, and it was a lovely gesture by Kath.
Preston won 4–2. Jean Lane became 1957's leading goalscorer, the
fifth consecutive season she had pulled off this feat.

Although 'Pop' was seriously ill, he had heard that Edna
Broughton (his little star) was considering leaving the club and
he was most concerned at the prospect of losing her. He wrote to
Edna on 26 February 1957 saying:

> I have really had another shock, and believe me I have had
> a few this last twelve months, one on top of the other. But
> I ask you, Edna, while I live you will carry on. You know
> what I think of you and you all know I have had a very
> serious illness that has taken all the starch out of me.
> Actually the doctor would have liked me to pack up
> everything. I have not been able to look after my own
> business for a very long time, never mind the football.
> Mrs Frankland has had to look after me and on top of it all
> we both had the flu together. I wondered when it was all
> going to end. Now Edna forget about leaving us, while I am
> head you stay. Remember just this Edna, I love my football
> and you know that as long as I am the manager I want my
> little star to stop with me, I cannot say more. But take this
> as final. I could not release you from my club. That is my
> regard for you.

Alfred Frankland died on 9 October 1957. He was seventy-five.
He had been taken ill again earlier in the year and his health had
been adversely affected by the death of his wife in July, as she had
been nursing him at home. He was cremated at Carleton, near
Blackpool.

During his forty-year association with Dick, Kerr Ladies, the team
played 748 games of football, won 702, drew thirty-three and lost
only thirteen. And they had raised somewhere in the region of
£150,000 for charity.

10 Joan Whalley

Joan played for Dick, Kerr's for almost twenty years. She signed for them when she was just fifteen years old and remembers that, following her joining the team, every time she came home from school there were reporters at her front door.

'I'd heard of Dick, Kerr Ladies before I ever wanted to join them. I was the only girl round by where I lived who played football. I used to wonder about Dick, Kerr's and how you got to play for them. Then, one day I went up to my auntie's, who lived on Watling Street Road, and she asked me to go to the fruit shop round the corner to get her some apples. When I got to the shop I didn't realize it was Frankland who was serving me, but somehow we got talking about football. I said I really wanted to join this Dick, Kerr Ladies team because I played football but didn't know how to get in touch with them. "Well," he said, "you've come to the right place. I'm the manager of Dick, Kerr Ladies football team, and my name is Alfred Frankland."

'After I met him I went dashing home, of course, and went rushing into the house: "Mother, Mother, I've met Mr Frankland, Dick, Kerr's manager and I might be playing for them."'

Joan realized her dream and made her debut for Dick, Kerr Ladies on Coronation Day, 12 May 1937, at Roundhay Park, Leeds. There was a big celebration to commemorate the coronation of King George VI, and there was a large crowd there. 'It was fantastic,' recalls Joan, 'I was at the end of the line when we all marched out on to the field. They played the national anthem and all the crowd were cheering, it was wonderful, it was out of this world. I think I scored that day, I'm not sure, but I know I was a very happy person.'

Joan Whalley was born in Preston on 18 December 1921, and she was probably one of the best women footballers of her time. She was always a bit of a tomboy and loved to play football with the boys as a youngster. Her father had bought her first pair of football boots when she was just five years old. He was convinced that his new baby was going to play football because of all the kicking it was doing even before being born!

She went to Deepdale Modern School at the same time as Tom Finney and they became good friends. Tom Finney, affectionately known in Preston as 'Sir Tom', was to become one of the best wingers Preston and England had ever seen. With seventy-seven caps for England and playing for only one club, his beloved Preston North End, Tom is one of the finest gentlemen of the game, as he never received a referee's caution throughout the whole of his playing career. Joan and Tom used to play football together on Waverley Park, and Joan remembers these things in particular of her 'kick-abouts' with Tom.

'One time, Tom had broken his arm and I had a septic finger. My mum kept putting a hot poultice on it for me and she put my arm in a sling. So Tom came round for me with his arm in a sling as well and he said, "Shall we go for a kick-around, Joan?" "Yes," I said, "Come on." So off we went on Waverley Park, the two of us with our arms in slings, kicking a ball about; we must have looked a right pair. We must have only been about thirteen years old at the time.

'I used to go to birthday parties at his house when we were all kids together, and I would say to him, "What do you want to do most, Tom?" and he would say, "I want to play for North End." I told him that I wanted to play for Dick, Kerr Ladies. Then eventually I did get to play for Dick, Kerr's and he got to play for North End, so we both got what we wanted. But of course, as we grew up, our lives took different paths and we didn't see one another again until years later at one of our matches played at Kirkham. They invited Tom to be our guest celebrity for the day because we always had a famous person to "kick off" or referee at our games. They were taking Tom down the line, introducing him to all the players and officials. When they reached me, I put out my hand to shake hands with my old friend, and I said with a smile, "Hiya champ", and he smiled back at me and said, "Hiya champ". It was a lovely moment.

'I always admired Tom because he never got big-headed about his success; his head always stayed the same size, so it meant he kept his feet right. I always said that if your head gets too big, your feet will get out of proportion. You should never get big headed about football.'

Both Joan and Tom played on the wing and it was said at the time that England could boast the best two right-wingers in the country, male and female. Joan was an excellent player, she was indeed the 'Tom Finney' of women's football, but in keeping with her own philosophy, she too kept her feet in proportion.

I first met Joan at her home in Carnforth. She told me she was not used to talking, as she had become something of a hermit during her years living alone on 'her mountain'. She had, from choice, dropped out from society because, as she says, 'I wanted to find a place where I could escape from this world of cruelty.' She wanted to be alone with only her animals for company and she advertised every week in the local papers – 'Lady with dogs requires semi-derelict, isolated cottage or farmhouse. Prepared to do it up.'

Long before Joan felt the need to leave her home, it had already become an animal sanctuary. She was well known for the work she did with stray animals, and every night when she arrived home from work there would be some child standing on her front doorstep with tears streaming down its cheeks and a tiny furry object wrapped up in a blanket. 'Please Joan, can you take it, my dad says it has to go.' Dogs, cats, rabbits; all had to be given homes, and seven o'clock seemed to be surgery time. Joan would bathe and bandage cut legs on dogs and cats, delouse flea-ridden pets, and doctor them up as best she knew. All the kids came from a big estate, where there was no money, so they could not afford vet's fees, consequently, each week it would cost Joan a small fortune replacing ointment, bandages and worm tablets.

Her house was full to overflowing, and at one point she had nine dogs, six grown cats, seventeen kittens, one tortoise, two budgies and two rabbits. She would write large notices and display them in her front windows – 'Good homes for puppies, good homes for kittens'. There was always someone standing outside her home reading her notices, and one such person, a friend called Doris, brought her an Alsation puppy called Hobo. It was a mindless vandal's savage and senseless treatment of this dog that finally drove Joan to sell her Preston home and move to an isolated spot on top of the Belmont Moors near Bolton. It was during the summer of 1975 that she went to live on 'her mountain', in a run-down cottage which had none of the things we all take for granted. She had no heating or hot running water, no bath, toilet, sink, cooker or fridge, and she had only one cold water tap which would often freeze up in the wintertime. Her only luxury was an electricity supply which consisted of two electric lights, one kettle and a black-and-white television. These were her only home comforts.

So Joan began her life in a remote wilderness with only her animals for companionship. Joan named her home OLCOTE Animal Sanctuary. OLCOTE stands for Our Little Corner Of The Earth.

She finally left 'her mountain' in 1988 at the age of sixty-seven, because she could hardly walk as a result of having a bad fall. She says 'It was very difficult for me to make the decision to leave. I had to find new homes for all my animals and it broke my heart to part with them, but I knew they would all be well cared for. It was a sad day when I left the mountain; I feel as though that's when my life ended.

'I can't have animals where I live now, but I'm surrounded by pictures of them. I owned my own house before I went up on the mountain, I used to earn a good wage to be able to keep everything going. I haven't got two ha'pennys to rub together now; it's all gone on my animals. I've spent all my lot on animals but we've all been very happy. I'm a real pauper now you know, I've bugger all, nothing in my life.

'When you are young, your life is full and you never have a minute, but when you get older and there's not much in your life, well, you drift back into the past and relive all the happy times. It keeps me cheerful because I never go out any more.'

Asked to share some more memories of her footballing days with Dick, Kerr Ladies, Joan reminisced at length.

'The game I remember most is when I played for Wales. We were on tour with the French team and the French were to play against Wales. For some reason they said Wales could have three of our players and the French could have three. The Welsh chose me as one of their players and played me at centre-forward. I wore a green shirt with a big red dragon across the back. I thought the dragon was wonderful, I loved it.

'They told me not to speak during the game because of course I didn't have a Welsh accent. They said, "Don't open your mouth, don't say anything, keep your mouth shut." That wasn't a problem for me, as I didn't speak much when I was playing.

'I had a really good game that day and I scored a hat-trick for Wales. Well, as soon as the referee blew the final whistle, the crowd rushed on to the pitch, grabbed me and put me up on their shoulders. All these Welsh fellas were slapping me on the back saying, "Well done girl, well done", and "What a great game". I was just laughing and smiling, I daredn't open my mouth and they took me right up to the dressing-room door. I was doing nothing but grin the whole time because I had scored three goals, but when I got into the dressing room I asked one of the girls to help get my shirt off. She asked why and I told her I daredn't move because it felt like all the skin was peeling off my back. I had very fine skin with being blonde and there were finger marks all down my back to my waist. I was red raw with all the slapping.

'When I got home my mum was asking how we had gone on. I told her all about it then I asked if she would put some cold cream or something on my back. When she saw it she said, "My God, I've never seen a back like that in all my life." There had been so many people slapping me that day they had taken all the skin off. Now, when I watch them on television at Wembley on Cup Final day and see them all going up the stairs to receive their medals, and everyone is slapping them on their back, it makes me cringe to remember it.

'I remember another time when we had all been up to play a match in Workington so it would be late at night when we would be getting home. We always had the same driver on our bus; his name was Tommy, and whenever we wanted to stop for a drink or go to the toilet, someone would shout, "Bispham, Bispham Tommy", and Tommy would always stop for us.

'Well, after this match in Workington someone shouted, "Bispham Tommy", and he pulled up at a pub and "Pop" was saying, "Now girls, we'll not be stopping long." The girls, of course, had other ideas and all the older players stopped quite a while having a few beers. "Pop" was trying to hurry them along and when he finally got them all out, we set off again.

'They were all quite tiddly and Lily Parr was well away. I don't know how many she'd had, but after we had been travelling about five miles or so, Parr shouts, "Stop this bloody bus." I always sat at the front near Tommy and I said to him, "There's something wrong, Parr's shouting to stop the bus." Tommy pulled over at the roadside and Parr said, "I'll have to get out, I'm going to be sick." After a while we all got back on the bus and after travelling another five miles or so, Parr shouts again, "Stop this bloody bus, stop this bloody bus." "Not again," said Tommy. So he pulled over to the side of the road and Parr said to him, "You'll have to go back, I've left my bloody false teeth."

'Tommy turned the bus around and he asked me if I could remember where we had stopped. I said I had a good idea, so off we went driving down the road looking for a pile of sick and Parr's teeth, and would you believe it but we found them! We wrapped them up in some paper and put them in her pocket. It was a while before she lived it down.

'There was never really any rivalry at the club; we all played for each other, but I always got the feeling that Margaret Thornborough never liked me. I have always got on with people wherever I've been, but the very first time I met her she seemed very cool and distant. I thought, never mind, she'll be all right when she gets to know me, but she never was. Even when we all worked together at Whittingham Hospital it was just the same.

'One time when we all worked at the hospital, a Saturday match came up and everyone else had managed to get the day off except for me, and I couldn't get a change of shift from anywhere. I had been all round the girls asking them to swap days off, I even tried to bribe them, I tried everything, but I couldn't get that day off for love nor money.

'The other girls in the team asked what I was going to do, so I told them I was just going to take the day off. They were very surprised and said, "You can't do that, there will be hell to play when you get back to work," but I said, "To hell with it, I don't care, I'll stand that, I'm not missing this match." I had never missed a game before and I wasn't going to miss one now.

'I took the day off, played the match, played a blinder and scored six goals. It was one of those days when everything went right. I went in to work the next day and I was waiting for the bombshell, but nothing happened. It was a relief to learn that matron was off for two days, and I thought, brilliant!

'On the Monday, the match report was in the paper. It was a long report and it was all about this brilliant performance by Joan Whalley, scoring six goals. On Tuesday, when I went in to work, the ward sister came up to me to tell me the matron wanted to see me in her office. I thought, "Oh hell, she's back, this is it."

'When I went in to her office I was trembling because in those days matrons were like dragons and my stomach was turning over and over. But I thought, "Never mind, I don't care, at least I played football," but I did think I would lose my job because of it. I really thought she would give me the sack.

'I walked in her office and stood at her desk. She pushed this newspaper cutting across to me and said, "Read that." There was a silence in the room and you could feel the tension. I pretended I hadn't seen it before and started reading it. All the time my stomach was churning over and she said, "You had a good game." My knees were knocking and I was in a terrible state; she must have been able to see I was terrified. I said, "Yes, Matron." "Well," she said, "I am not going to do anything about it, I am not going to put you on suspension, I am not going to do anything at all."

'Someone had put the article in an envelope and left it in her office for her to read. "I do not like anonymous letters," she went on, "and if the person concerned did not have the courage to put her name to the bottom of this, I do not want to know anything about it." She just pushed it to one side and said, "You can go." I had never been so relieved in all my life.

'I can never be sure who it was, but I always believed in my mind that it was Margaret Thornborough because I knew that she never really liked me. But whoever it was, they did me a big favour. If matron had found out any other way about me taking the day off, who knows what would have happened to me?

'I was lucky when I was playing because I never really had any injuries. I put my cartilage out and odd bits like that, but they just pushed those back. "Pop" always used to tell the girls to go to his house for a soda bath. They were marvellous for getting rid of all your aches and pains. You get your bath water nice and hot and put a couple of tea cups of ordinary washing soda into the bath, and have a good long soak in it. Don't rub yourself because the soda will bring your skin off, just swill the water all over yourself and soak for about half an hour. When you've finished, pat yourself dry, and when you've done that, if you have anyone who can give you a gentle massage with a bit of warm olive oil, it will work wonders. When you get up the next day, all your aches and pains will have disappeared.

'A friend in Bolton once invited me over to have what she called, "a proper soda bath" from the trainer of Bolton Wanderers FC. She said, "He will show you how it's done, he puts the footballers through it and he is really good with it."

'When I got there, he ran a bath – his wife was hovering about in the background – and he said, "If you are nervous keep your panties on and get in this bath." He had put one and a half pounds of washing soda in the water, and told me to just lie there. His wife was there with a stopwatch; it's as drastic as that. It was six minutes for a woman and eight minutes for a man. He was swilling the water all over my body and the sweat was stinging

Joan Whalley gives her team talk.
Left to right: Joan Burke, Joan Whalley, Betty Sharples,
Peggy Sharples, June Gregson, Jean Lane.
Seated: Muriel Heaney, Jean Dent.

me, it was like being in a sauna. Next thing, his wife clicked the stopwatch and said, "Right, six minutes." He told me to get out and when I put my hands on the side of the bath to get out, I couldn't move. I said, "I can't move," and he started laughing. He was a great big burly fella with big muscles and he just lifted me out of the bath, put me on a table and covered me with a great big bath towel. He must have used about six towels putting them on and patting me dry and the sweat was coming off me, I was steaming hot. I thought, "Dear God, what has he put in it?"

'When I finally dried off he dusted me all over with talcum powder, wrapped me up in a light blanket and put me into bed. His wife brought me a nice cup of hot sweet tea and said, "Drink that, then you are going to sleep for four hours." There wasn't an ounce of energy left in me, and I couldn't believe it, and I did go to sleep for four hours like she said I would.

'When I woke up he asked me how I felt, and I said, "To put it bluntly, absolutely buggered." He told me I would feel like that for at least another five days. I couldn't believe it, but he knew we had a game the following Saturday and he had planned it so that I had five complete days before the next match. I was tired all week because of it, but come the match on Saturday, nothing could stop me. Three goals, no messing, it was brilliant stuff, I played a blinder. His soda bath had obviously done the trick, but he said, "Don't ever try this on your own, you must have it done under medical supervision. I am qualified so it was all right."

'It was a wonderful life, the games we played, the travelling, being part of a team, and even though we were never allowed to play on league grounds, there were always thousands of people who turned up to watch us play. There are so many wonderful memories.

'I remember the good times we used to have when we were going home on the bus after an away match. Nancy Thomson played an accordion and there were two or three of us who played a mouth organ. We all used to team up together and have a sing-song, they were happy times. Annie Lynch was a marvellous singer; she and her friend used to harmonize all the old songs like "Smile awhile" and things like that.

'Yes, we had a great time, it was a wonderful life and I don't regret one minute of it. If I had my time over I would to it all again.'

11 The Final Whistle

Following the death of Alfred Frankland, his son Ronald expected the team to fold up, but the girls objected to this. They called a meeting and asked Kath Latham if she would take on the new role of running the club. As she had been doing most of the work during 'Pop's' illness, she willingly accepted the job. Doreen Gibbon, who played in the team at the time, helped Kath and acted as assistant manager for a couple of years.

'When I took over,' Kath recalls, 'there was nothing except for an old scrapbook, and we even had to pinch that because Ron had destroyed everything. There was no correspondence, no address book, no record books, nothing, absolutely nothing. We didn't even know who the organizers of the matches were, we had to start from scratch. We had to rely on someone having some old programmes which had some information, then find a telephone directory for that area and hope they were listed. That's how I had to start because there was nothing left.'

It is surely strange that this should have happened. Someone credited as being the 'Father of Women's Football', and responsible for raising £150,000 for charity, might reasonably have expected his family to be so proud of his achievements that they would want the world to know about them? Why, then, were the books destroyed?

The team had quite a number of games with Accrington Ladies until their disbandment, and several of the Accrington players came to play for Preston. One such was Val Walsh. Val was about sixteen or seventeen at the time, and Kath says, 'Matt Busby came to see one of our matches at Blackpool. He sat in the stands and said of Val Walsh that she was the best player he had ever seen in his life, and if she had been a man, he would have signed her up there and then to play for Manchester United! She was a marvellous player, and an excellent hockey player who went on to play for England at Wembley. Matt Busby asked us how we went about obtaining our footballs, and we told him that we had to beg, borrow or steal them. The following week one arrived through the post. It had only been used once by the Manchester United players. We were all delighted.'

The players used to provide their own football kit, but eventually the club raised enough money to buy a new strip. After a couple of years they had enough in club funds to buy a second strip, and had an embroidered badge designed to wear on the shirts. They also had some blazer badges made, which made their appearance a credit to the club's good name.

Under Kath Latham's guidance they played every week from May through to October. Kath remembers 'We played at more places than "Pop" did. He tended only to play Manchester and Littlewood's Ladies, unless on tour with the French team. Perhaps as he was getting older the travelling became too much for him. Accrington Ladies tried to get some fixtures with us, but for some reason "Pop" wouldn't let us play against them.

'When I was running things we would play Foden's from Cheshire and Handy Angles from the Midlands, as well as the other local fixtures. The Isle of Man was an annual fixture, played during the French tour. They used to go by boat from Fleetwood on a Thursday morning, play the match on Thursday night, stay over, then come back on Friday. After I took over, I wrote to the charity organizers in the Isle of Man and suggested that it might be cheaper if we flew from Blackpool in the morning, played the fixture, then flew back at night, as it would save them the expense of overnight accommodation for two teams. We contacted Blackpool airport, who said we could have a day flight but the departure time from Ronaldsway airport was 6 p.m., and as that was the same time as the start of our match, it was no good for us. Eventually, they very kindly agreed to delay the flight until 9 p.m. as we were only five minutes from the airport at Castletown. The pilot used to come to the match, so we always knew that the plane wouldn't go without us! It was a mad rush though because Blackpool airport closed at 10 p.m. It saved a lot of money in expenses, and by doing it that way, the charity we were playing for asked us to play two games for them, one in July and one in August, so we got an extra fixture out of it.

'I arranged quite a lot of matches for cancer research; in each case it was for a local committee and the proceeds went direct to that particular area. We went to Buckley in Flintshire. It was our

The team with their new team manager, Kath Latham, 1959.
Back (left to right): Barbara Prescot, Barbara Widdows, Ann Lymath, Pauline Rimmer, Pat Preece, Kath Latham.

Front (left to right): Joan Whalley, Irene Lydiate, Jean Lane, Edna Broughton, Doreen Espley, Joan Euxton.

first fixture there and it was a great success. After the game we were asked if we would play again the following year.

'I always liked to make sure we had a drink somewhere after the game and we found a quiet little pub in Buckley which had a few of the regulars in who were all sat there with long faces. In those days, there was always a piano in the pubs and I would usually start playing a few tunes and my sister, who had a marvellous voice, would get all the team singing. We did this in the pub in Buckley, the drinks started flowing and we were having a marvellous time, and within half an hour the place was packed out!

'When we returned the following year, we said we would go back to the same pub after our meal. When we got there the place was full; they were all in there waiting for us to arrive! That's what it was like, we always drew in the crowds, we would raise the roof wherever we stopped. And it was the same on the coach afterwards on the way home.

'It was something that "Pop" was always very much against, until later on, just before he died. But we put our foot down and told him that we were stopping somewhere. We had given up our Saturday and our free time, so we were entitled to enjoy ourselves after the game. He always lost out because we would say that we wouldn't come to the next match if he didn't let us stop.'

Jean Lane has fond memories of the after-match singing sessions: 'We would all be singing and Kath would be playing the piano. She could make a piano talk, could Kath. We always used to sing a song called "How Can I Leave You", and whenever I hear it now, it brings back many happy memories.

> How can I leave you though I know it's time to go
> How can I leave you when I love you so
> Eventide is falling, I must be on my way
> All the world is calling, but my heart says stay
> Faithful for ever, my love will be a star
> Shining for ever, everywhere you are.'

Towards the end of the 1950s, Kath was advertising for players once again and Joan Briggs was a player who travelled from Stockwell, London, to play for the team. It would be four in the morning before she arrived back at Euston station!

By the start of the 1960s, the team claimed to have raised £175,000 for charity, having played 786 games, won 689, drawn forty-two and lost sixteen.

Major signings in the early 1960s were Freda Garth and Sheila Porter. As Mrs Sheila Parker, she went on to captain England and has won every honour possible in women's football. Sheila is probably the last active link with Preston (Dick, Kerr) Ladies. She continued to play football in the North West Women's Regional Football League up to the mid-1990s. She is also a qualified referee and regularly officiates at both men's and women's matches in the north west.

In 1962 the dinosaurs at the FA were to show the full extent of their opposition to the women's game when they stopped two games between Dick, Kerr's and Oldham Ladies from going ahead. The Welsh FA banned a game from taking place in Rhyl, with prospects of a 10,000 gate of the year at Rhyl's football ground. The *Daily Mail* reported that the idea of staging a female soccer 'derby' on a Welsh ground came from Mr Ken Hughes, vice-chairman of the Flintshire Fire Services Benevolent Fund. He was sure it would be a real winner, with Whit Monday as the day chosen for the charity match. But when Mr Hughes wrote to the headquarters of the FA of Wales, he was told: 'Ladies' soccer. Nothing doing.' The Secretary of the Welsh FA said, 'Our rule book prohibits ladies football on any ground affiliated to the association. We think that football is a man's game and that there is no place for lady players.'

In Lancashire, it was the same story. The LFA stopped the match from taking place at the British Legion ground, at Newton near Wigan, also between Dick, Kerr's and Oldham Ladies, in aid of the Wigan Society for the Blind. The ground was also used by Wigan Rovers AFC, who played in the Lancashire Combination League, and they were told by the FA that they would be in serious trouble, and even face suspension, if they allowed the game to go ahead. Despite the fact that the tickets had been printed and posters had been put up advertising the game, the FA refused to give way on the matter and the game was rearranged to be played at Christopher Park, Wigan. A spokesman for the Blind Society, Mr Oswald Johns, was quoted in the *Manchester Evening News* on 30 August 1962: 'The reason given by the FA for their decision, is that women are not allowed to play on any FA ground. In fairness, it should be understood that the Legion ground is only rented to Wigan Rovers, and in the opinion of the Newton British Legion, the FA have no jurisdiction whatsoever over the match.' He added, 'The LFA's decision is archaic. It is a Victorian hangover.'

In spite of the FA's action, they attracted a crowd of several thousand, and after the match handed over a large cheque to the charity.

By 1963, the tide was beginning to turn for the club and they were beaten 3–1 at home by Foden's. And in the return match played at York, they managed only a 0–0 draw. At the end of the season, they once more had to advertise for new players, but it was becoming increasingly difficult to recruit young blood to replace the older, experienced players who had come to the end of their careers with the team. They played sixteen games in 1963, won ten, drew three and lost three.

In 1964 they played only twelve games, but there was talk of making plans for the fiftieth anniversary of the club in 1967. It was difficult for Kath to keep things going, as it was virtually impossible to find new players, and the ones they did have were scattered so widely. There were girls from Preston, Wigan, Chorley, Southport and Manchester, and they never knew when any of them would fail to turn up for a match. They could never get together for a training session, either, and in fact the only time some of them met up was when they arrived in the changing room for the match.

In 1965 they had only three fixtures arranged, all against Handy Angles from the Midlands. The first game they drew 4–4. For their second match they had only nine players in the first half, but finished the game with ten. They still won by 5–1. The last match of the 1965 season was against Handy Angles on 21 August. They won 4–0, in what turned out to be the last ever game in this famous club's history. Their first score line in those far-off days of 1917 was also a 4–0 victory, and so it was fitting that they should end in the way they had begun.

No one knew at this stage, of course, that this *was* to be their last match, but later in the year all the players received a letter from Kath Latham saying that the club was to fold owing to the lack of players. There must have been a great sadness among them all, especially the older members of the team who would not have the opportunity to play again.

Kath felt it was better to end the team, after forty-eight years of the club's existence, so that the name of Preston (Dick, Kerr) Ladies would be remembered as one of the top teams in the world, one which kept all appointments and fielded a full team in each match. The support from the public had never waned; their problems were all due to a lack of players. They were no longer able to field a team that could live up to the club's proud name. It was a difficult decision for Kath to make, one about which she was upset. It must have taken a lot of soul-searching. Above all others, she knew the history of this world-famous club, she knew the importance of what she had inherited after 'Pop' Frankland's death, but there did not seem to be any alternative. After all the glory, after all the cheers, the euphoria and the fame, the end came quietly, and a giant was laid to rest.

Throughout the club's long history, they received over 160 civic receptions, and the official records state that they raised somewhere in the region of £175,000 for charity. The actual amount will never be known.

Their impressive playing record reads: played 828, won 758, drew forty-six and lost only twenty-four games in forty-eight years. They scored over 3,500 goals.

They set a standard that will never be equalled, and the town of Preston can be proud of where it all began.

Jean Lane said, 'It was a privilege to play for them. They talk today about what it means to put on an England shirt, but it's no more a privilege for them than it was for us to wear a Dick, Kerr shirt; they were a great team.'

In 1966 England won the World Cup and football mania swept the country. Everyone wanted to play football and there was no shortage of girls wanting to take up the game. The Women's Football Association was formed in 1969, and the FA eventually gave way to public opinion and finally recognized women's football in 1971, fifty years after they had banned it, when the WFA was granted county status. The WFA administered all its own affairs until 1993, when it was disbanded and the FA took over responsibility for women's football.

It is doubtful, though, if the players of today could ever fill a stadium to its capacity, as the pioneers of women's football did on so many occasions. This is not because today's players are any less capable, but the damage done by the FA all those years ago may probably never really be undone. But we have a lot to thank them for, those wonderful women who fought so valiantly against all adversity, to play the game of football for its own sake.

Afterword

Dick, Kerr Ladies were reunited for the first time since the team's disbandment on Sunday 2 August 1992. The reunion took place as part of an International Women's Football Tournament, the Preston Guild Lancashire Trophy, seventy-five years after the team's amazing beginnings. All in all, I managed to locate seventeen players, and fourteen of them were able to meet up for the first time in over thirty years. We entertained them to a VIP champagne reception in what turned out to be a very emotional evening. The *Lancashire Evening Post* reported their reunion as part of the Preston Guild Celebrations. The BBC saw the report and they came along to film the occasion. In spite of the length of time since they had last kicked a ball together, Dick, Kerr Ladies turned back the clock to show the strength of their pulling power. The mere mention of their name after all these years was still big news.

Some of the ladies were able to come along during the day to watch the football, and it was a big thrill for them to be part of the women's game again and everybody wanted to meet them. They thoroughly enjoyed watching the girls competing for the Preston Guild Lancashire Trophy, but of course they all thought that they had played the best football in their day! In those days of course, they played with the old heavy leather ball, which would retain the wet when it was raining and would require a lot of force behind the kick to lift it. Joan Whalley said, 'Nowadays the footballs are wonderful. I managed to get the chance to kick one today and I thought it was marvellous. I wish they would have had those when I was playing.'

We had to keep the film crew a secret from Joan. She is really quite a shy lady who would rather avoid the limelight, and had she known what was in store, she might not have come. We did not tell her about the cameras until she arrived for the champagne reception, by which time it was too late for her to get away! No one had seen Joan for years. They had heard she had 'dropped out' from society and become something of a recluse, but knew little of her life or whereabouts.

What an emotion-packed night it turned out to be for 'my ladies'! It was wonderful to watch them greet one another with hugs, kisses and tears of joy, and as they talked about 'the good old days', the years just seemed to melt away in their memories. They were youngsters again, reliving old times, and the champagne was flowing as they celebrated their long-overdue reunion.

To add a civic flavour to the proceedings, the Mayor of the Borough of Wyre, Mr Tom Ibison, came along to offer an official welcome to everyone on behalf of Wyre Borough Council.

Together for the very first time in all those years were: Joan Whalley, Dorothy Whalley, Edna Clayton, Joan Burke, Frances Appleby, Marjorie Foulkes, Audrey Coupe, Muriel Heaney, June Gregson, Jean Lane, Brenda Keen, Barbara Prescott, Sheila Parker and Barbara Widdows.

Joan Whalley was interviewed by Christine Talbot, the BBC reporter, who asked her how long it had been since they met. Joan said, 'It's been over thirty years since I saw any of these girls and I have thoroughly enjoyed meeting them all. It's like meeting old friends over again. None of us have been in contact, but over the last few minutes it's been like travelling back in time for thirty years. It's a wonderful feeling. You get very lonely when you get older, you miss all the girls, you miss the comradeship. It's a wonderful thing really when you are all in a team.' Frances Appleby said, 'It's lovely to see them all again, I've looked forward to this night for weeks and weeks.'

June Gregson was reunited with her best friend Barbara Prescott. They always used to sit with one another on the bus while travelling to and from matches. June had a lump in her throat as she said, 'Coming back and seeing all these people here today is absolutely fantastic and I miss it.'

I was choked with emotion as I saw just how much the night meant to them all. I was so proud of 'my ladies' and it was a privilege to have met them. I did not see any of them as old ladies, I saw them as footballers; we were as one.

Their arrival to the main function room was announced and the present-day women footballers gave them a standing ovation as they came in to take their seats. The cheers and applause given to these ladies from the greatest era of the women's game was literally deafening. It was a fitting tribute to them and what they had achieved so long ago. The world famous Dick, Kerr Ladies were back together!

After the cabaret, which they all thoroughly enjoyed, we had arranged a special surprise presentation to honour them and to commemorate their reunion in Guild year. We gave each of them a copper engraving of a Preston scene with the inscription, 'PRESENTED TO DICK, KERR LADIES, PRESTON GUILD 1992'.

I introduced them all to the audience individually and brought them on to the stage one by one. Each was given a rapturous welcome from the girls who had competed for the Preston Guild Lancashire Trophy, and they were touched by the warmth of their reception.

Edna Clayton, at seventy-eight years of age, was the oldest member of the team present on the night. I informed everyone of this as Edna came up to receive her award, and an extra-loud cheer was given to her. Edna raised her right arm in acknowledgement as she gracefully accepted the applause.

I saved Joan Whalley until last so that the Dick, Kerr girls could join with us all in applauding her on to the stage. I knew they all had a deep respect for her and I wanted her to see just how much regard everyone felt for her, and to give her an extra-special accolade as one of the finest players ever to turn out for Dick, Kerr Ladies. In women's football she is a legend in her own lifetime.

It was a wonderful moment for her, receiving the applause of her peers, and the whole room erupted with cheers, whistles and applause for this truly remarkable woman. She modestly accepted it, while wondering what all the fuss was about.

After all the presentations had been made, to mark the end of the competition, one of the girls, Maria Harper from Merseyside, who plays for Knowsley United (now Liverpool WFC), did her usual annual party piece and sang a song for us. Maria is a talented football player and a popular young woman full of that wonderful Scouse humour, who is not afraid of the limelight.

This year, Maria dedicated her song to Dick, Kerr Ladies. The song she sang was, 'Those were the Days', and the whole room joined in with her to pay their own tribute to these very special ladies. 'Those were the days my friend, we thought they'd never end, those were the days, oh yes those were the days.'

It was a truly memorable occasion, which I am sure held many moments for all of them to treasure. They were asked for autographs, and many of the girls wanted to have their photographs taken with *the* Dick, Kerr ladies. They said they were treated like royalty and it was nothing more than they deserved. They all swapped addresses and pledged to keep in touch. The ladies from the greatest era of women's football were back together, and the name of which they were all so proud will live on.

The whole event, however, was soon to be tinged with sadness. The next day, Edna Clayton was taken to hospital, seriously ill, and on Tuesday 4 August, she passed away. Everyone was so shocked and upset at the suddenness of her passing and none of us could really believe it.

It was a strange feeling for me. I had felt a closeness with Edna, a feeling of belonging that usually comes only with knowing a person for many years. I feel like that with all of 'my ladies', and it seemed too soon to be saying goodbye and mourning any of them. We had only just begun to get to know one another. Apparently, Edna had not been well for some time and it was touch and go whether she came to the reunion at all. I am so very glad she did, and I am sure she was too.

Death is an inevitability for all of us and I suppose we all hope we can go with some kind of dignity. Edna had that, and the last night out of her life was spent celebrating the achievements of Dick, Kerr Ladies, something which was a big part of her life in days gone by. Before she died, she had the recognition of her part in this world-famous team and for that, at least, we can all be grateful.

As a result of the reunion, Frances Appleby and Joan Whalley were able to renew their old friendship and now write to each other every week. They used to live a few streets away from one another when they were younger, but like most people they lost touch. Now they regularly catch up on the past years and share memories from the good old days and their hopes for tomorrow.

Brenda Eastwood took charge of keeping them all in touch and hoped to arrange meetings every few months or so. Their next get together was another huge success, held at the Unicorn public house in Preston. I was invited along to be with them all and, as I sat listening to them reminiscing about their days from the golden era of women's football, it was wonderful to see how happy they were by just being together again.

I was unaware that they had secretly held a collection for me, and in one of the proudest moments of my life, they presented me with a trophy to show their appreciation of being reunited.

It said, 'TO GAIL, PRESTON GUILD 1992, COMMEMORATING THE REUNION OF DICK, KERR LADIES FC'. I had a big lump in my throat, I was speechless. I was searching for the right words to try to convey just how much their reunion had meant to me and how much they had all come to mean to me personally. I felt humble in their presence, and I knew in my heart that Dick, Kerr Ladies would be a part of me for the rest of my life, for without their gallant efforts none of this would have been possible.

I have tried to write this book in their honour, to dedicate it to each and every one of those wonderful women who, throughout their forty-eight-year dominance of the game, have left us with such a remarkable legacy. They have shown the world just how much can be achieved, even when all the odds are stacked against you.

The enormity of what they actually did achieve can at last be appreciated by those of us who have reaped the rewards of their endeavours. Not just the thousands of women who play football in this country today, but the countless tens of thousands of men, women and children, the sick, the lame and the dying, who benefited because of these women who gave so much to help those in need.

Joan Whalley said, 'But for this book, all the old members of Dick, Kerr Ladies would go to their graves forgotten for ever, but this will keep us all alive in the pages of history.' Now their families and future generations will know of their incredible success story. They can take their rightful place in the Sporting Hall of Fame, for Dick, Kerr Ladies Football Club undoubtedly are, In a League of Their Own!

Dick, Kerr Ladies Football Club 1917–65 Roll of Honour

Lydia Ackers
Frances Appleby
Sheila Appleby
Elsie Arnold
Lizzy Ashcroft

Audrey Bagot
Carol Barber
Marion Barker
Dorothy Barnett
Kath Barrington
Pamela Barrington
Kath Bartley
Joan Billington
E. Birkins
Leila Boardman
Miss Booth
Joan Briggs (Hall)
Stella Briggs
Edna Broughton
Joan Burke
Jean Butcher
E. Buxton
Lily Buxton

Lesley Caldwell
Joan Carruthers
Doris Carter
Mary Carter
Pat Catterall
Sue Chorley

Sheila Clague
Elsie Clarke
Joan Clay
Daisy Clayton
E. Clayton
Edna Clayton
Glenys Cocker
Florence Coles
Yvonne Cooper
Violet Coulton
Audrey Coupe
Daphne Coupe
Edith Cox
Miss Crawshaw
Annie Crozier
Bessie Cunliffe

Barbara Dandy
Louie Davies
Jean Dent
M. Dent
Annie Derbyshire
Jacky Devaux
May Dickenson
Jessie Dickinson
Cissy Dixon
Margaret Dolderson
Miss Donoghue
Amy Duxbury
E. Duxbury

Dorothy Eastwood
Joan Eckton
Pat Ellis
Margaret Empgrave
Doreen Espley
Joan Euxton

Joan Fairclough
S. Fairclough
Frances Foulkes
Marjorie Foulkes
J. Frankland

Diane Gant
Eva Gardner
R. J. Garrier
Freda Garth
Doreen Gibbon
Jean Gibson
Barbara Gilbert
Margery Giles
E. Glover
Mavis Glover
D. Gollin
Jean Gollin
Margaret Goodenson
May Graham
June Gregson
A. Grice
Emily Grice
Margaret Groom

Yvonne Hamer
Alice Hargreaves
Jennie Harris
Lily Harris
Florrie Haslam
Annie Hastie
Jean Hayes
Muriel Heaney
May Helme
Connie Hill

Anne Hodgkinson
Miss Hodgkinson
Dorothy Hodson
S. Holt
Alma Hopkins
C. Howarth
Lucy Hoyle
May Hoyle
Nellie Hoyle
Rosette Huard
Sally Hulme
Edith Hutton
Miss Hyton

Emily Jones
Lily Jones

M. Kay
Brenda Keen
Alice Kell
Sally Kendal
Stella Kendall
Miss Knowles

Jenny Lancaster
Jean Lane
Barbara Large
E. Latham
Kath Latham
Kath Lear
Lily Lee
Ann Lord
Kathleen Luke
Gladys Lunn
Irene Lydiate
Ann Lymath
Annie Lynch
Connie Lynch
G. Lyons
Minnie Lyons

Miss McAvoy
Bridget McCauley

Ann McGrath
Lorraine McKenna
Miss McLean
Miss Marsden
Annie Marsh
Lily Martin
Peggy Mason
Margaret Miller
Pat Miller
Alice Mills
Nellie Mitchell
Jean Moizer
Doris Morley
Hannah Morley

Hilda Nettle
Alice Newsham
May Newton
Doreen Nield
E. Nixon
Alice Norris
Doreen Norris

Mlle Ourry
Sue Owen

Sheila Parker (Porter)
A. Parkinson
F. Parkinson
Hilda Parkinson
Jean Parnell
Lily Parr
Miss Partington
Margaret Penberthy
Miss Perkins
Irene Philips
M. Pickering
Margaret Pickavant
Sheila Pinder
Joan Pomfret
Carmen Pomies

Marjorie Potter
E. Pragnall
Pat Preece
Barbara Prescott

F. Rance
Miss Rawsthorne
Florrie Redford
Doreen Richards
Miss Richards
E. Riegnall
Pauline Rimmer
Glenys Rostron

Dorothy Saycell
Polly Scott
Margaret Scratchley
Minnie Seed
C. Sharpe
Betty Sharples
Peggy Sharples
H. Shaw
Maggie Shaw
Grace Sibbert
Joan Spavin
A. Standing
Lily Stanley
Miss Streton
Irene Swift

Joan Tench
M. Thomas
Margaret Thornborough
Nancy Thomson
Elsie Tierney
B. Traynor

Miss Varley

Dorothy Wainwright
Molly Walker

Alice Walmsley
Jessie Walmsley
Val Walsh
Miss Waring
Dorothy Whalley
Joan Whalley
Sheila Whiteoak
Elizabeth Whittle
G. Whittle
Barbara Widdows

Joan Wilkinson
Pat Wilkinson
Rose Wilson
Alice Woods
E. Worrall
Lottie Worrall
Mary Worswick

Elsie Yates
Nellie Yates

One of the last team photos, 1959.
Back (left to right): Kath Latham, Pat Preece,
Irene Lydiate, Ann Lymath, Jean Gibson, Pauline Rimmer,
Glennis Cocker, Doreen Espley.
Front (left to right): Joan Whalley, Joan Briggs,
Jean Lane, Freda Garth, Mavis Glover.

Also available from Scarlet Press

Women on the Ball
A guide to women's football
Sue Lopez

Women on the Ball is the first book to cover all aspects of the women's game. It covers the early history to the present state of play around the world and provides profiles of the great women players, clubs and pioneers. It is an indispensable guide for any football enthusiast.

'Sue Lopez knows that raising awareness of the women's game is as much about creating a sense of heritage as getting people to go along and watch. Her book, always entertaining and informative, will do much to accomplish the first of those two things. **Buy it and be enlightened**.' *Goal Magazine* ***** 'Excellent, must have Book of the Month'

'It is heartening to see the author's genuine passion for her subject and it would be truly unfortunate if her call for action were to go unheeded.' *FA Gold* (in Association with Sports Pages)

'This is a fine useful handbook and ... a powerful political tract.' *On the Ball Magazine*

'As a history the book delivers a solid, factual base which will be useful in schools, colleges and universities. As a handbook it provides information on which, perhaps, a bigger and better women's game can be built.' *Times Educational Supplement*

'After reading this, no one will be able to deny how much some women have been, and are, "on the ball"' Lawrie McMemeny

'Sue Lopez brings an ideal perspective to the subject as both a former top flight player and now an admired coach.' John Morton, Chairman, English Schools' Football Association

288pp, 24 b/w illustrations
ISBN 1 85727 016 9